Low-Cost Local Area Networks

by

Stephen P.M. Bridges

 Publishers. Wilmslow

HALSTED PRESS a division of **JOHN WILEY & SONS**
New York · Chichester · Brisbane · Toronto

Copyright © Stephen P.M. Bridges 1986.

All Rights Reserved

No Part of this book may be reproduced or transmitted by any means without the prior permission of the publisher. The only exceptions are for the purposes of review, or as provided for by the Copyright (Photocopying) Act.

ISBN 0–905104–86–2 (Sigma Press)
ISBN 0–470–20758–2 (Halsted Press)

First published in 1986 by:
SIGMA PRESS
98A Water Lane
Wilmslow
Cheshire
U.K.

Published in 1986 in the U.S.A. and Canada by
HALSTED PRESS
A Division of JOHN WILEY & SONS INC.,
New York

Distributed in U.K., Europe and Africa by:
JOHN WILEY & SONS LIMITED
Baffins Lane, Chichester
West Sussex, England

Library of Congress CIP Data

Printed in Malta by Interprint Limited

CONTENTS

1. Introduction 1
   What are Local Area Networks? 2
   What does a Local Area Network do? 4
   Who uses Local Area Networks? 5
   Background Information 7

2. Types of Local Area Network 9
   Topology 9
      Star 9
      Loop 11
      Ring 12
      Bus 15
      Other topologies 17
   Access method 17
      Bus-sharing techniques 18
         CSMA/CD 18
         Token passing 20
      Ring access techniques 20
         Token passing 21
         Empty slot 22
         Buffer insertion 25
   Signalling method 27
      Baseband transmission 28
      Broadband transmission 28
   Transmission medium 31
      Twisted pair 32
      Ribbon/multicore cables 33
      Coaxial cable 33
      Fibre optics 34
   Transmission mode 36

3. Standards 39
   What use are standards? 39
   Standards 40
      Open system interconnections 40
      IEE 802 43

```
                Other standards bodies . . . . . . . . . . . . . . . . . . . . . . . 45
            De-facto standards . . . . . . . . . . . . . . . . . . . . . . . . . . . . . 45
                Ethernet . . . . . . . . . . . . . . . . . . . . . . . . . . . . . . . . . . . 45
                The Cambridge Ring . . . . . . . . . . . . . . . . . . . . . . . 46
                IBM token-passing ring . . . . . . . . . . . . . . . . . . . 47
            Future trends . . . . . . . . . . . . . . . . . . . . . . . . . . . . . . . . . 47

4. User Requirements: specifying and purchasing a LAN . . . . . . . . . . 49
            What do you want from a LAN? . . . . . . . . . . . . . . . . . . . . . . . 49
            Specifying a LAN . . . . . . . . . . . . . . . . . . . . . . . . . . . . . . . 51
            Matching LANs to users . . . . . . . . . . . . . . . . . . . . . . . . . . . 52
            Purchasing a LAN . . . . . . . . . . . . . . . . . . . . . . . . . . . . . . 56

5. Practical Installation . . . . . . . . . . . . . . . . . . . . . . . . . . . . . . . . 59
            Theory and practice . . . . . . . . . . . . . . . . . . . . . . . . . . . . . 59
            Common problems . . . . . . . . . . . . . . . . . . . . . . . . . . . . . . 59

6. Related Systems . . . . . . . . . . . . . . . . . . . . . . . . . . . . . . . . . . . 65
            PABX 65
            Intelligent terminal switches . . . . . . . . . . . . . . . . . . . . . . 70
            Wide area telephone networks . . . . . . . . . . . . . . . . . . . . . . 72

7. Research Networks . . . . . . . . . . . . . . . . . . . . . . . . . . . . . . . . . 75
            Ethernet . . . . . . . . . . . . . . . . . . . . . . . . . . . . . . . . . . . . . . 76
                Ethernet specification . . . . . . . . . . . . . . . . . . . . . . . 77
            Cambridge Ring . . . . . . . . . . . . . . . . . . . . . . . . . . . . . . . . 82
            Ethernet and the Cambridge Ring in the future . . . . . . . . . . . . 85

8. Proprietary LANs . . . . . . . . . . . . . . . . . . . . . . . . . . . . . . . . . . 87
            Econet . . . . . . . . . . . . . . . . . . . . . . . . . . . . . . . . . . . . . . 87
            Clearway . . . . . . . . . . . . . . . . . . . . . . . . . . . . . . . . . . . . 91
            Multilink . . . . . . . . . . . . . . . . . . . . . . . . . . . . . . . . . . . . 95
            V-Net . . . . . . . . . . . . . . . . . . . . . . . . . . . . . . . . . . . . . . 100
            IBM-PC Networks . . . . . . . . . . . . . . . . . . . . . . . . . . . . . 103
            Appletalk . . . . . . . . . . . . . . . . . . . . . . . . . . . . . . . . . . . . 107
            Infaplug . . . . . . . . . . . . . . . . . . . . . . . . . . . . . . . . . . . . 108
            Commodore Keynet . . . . . . . . . . . . . . . . . . . . . . . . . . . . 111
            The Amstrad Network . . . . . . . . . . . . . . . . . . . . . . . . . . . 113

9. Future trends . . . . . . . . . . . . . . . . . . . . . . . . . . . . . . . . . . . . 119
            Compatibility . . . . . . . . . . . . . . . . . . . . . . . . . . . . . . . . . 119
            Standards and the high-cost, low-cost split . . . . . . . . . . . . . 120
            Falling costs and chip sets . . . . . . . . . . . . . . . . . . . . . . . . 121
            Network-to-network connections . . . . . . . . . . . . . . . . . . . . 123
            General . . . . . . . . . . . . . . . . . . . . . . . . . . . . . . . . . . . . . 123
```

Appendix A: Available LANs. 125

Appendix B: Standards 165

Appendix C: Bibliography 167

Appendix D: Glossary of terms 169

Index 177

Chapter 1

Introduction

Local Area Networks (LANs) have burst upon the computing and engineering scene in recent years, as if from nowhere. In fact, like most other technical innovations, they are the product of long and careful development and the combination of many different established technologies. That they have commanded so much recent attention is an indication that there is a general need for them at this time. LANs can be seen as a solution to a problem, and awareness of this fact in a potential user of LANs prompts the questions: are they the best solution to MY problems, and, if so, which LAN is the best solution?

This book will attempt, with as little esoteric language as possible, to answer these questions. Its aims are:

>To explain LANs.
>To describe the technology involved.
>To indicate what LANs can (and cannot) do.
>To give an indication of where LANs stand in the computer technology marketplace.
>To give a comprehensive account of currently available systems.

We will be looking at LANs, not from a theoretical viewpoint, but rather as possible solutions to practical problems. However, no solution to a technical problem can be found without examining the technical background of the problem, and so there is a section in the book devoted to an explanation of the various technologies available and a comparison of their relative merits.

This book also contains detailed descriptions of a number of proprietary LANs, chosen for their low cost, wide applicability, or particular technical merits. 'Low-cost' is an extremely relative term and petty cash for one business may be a year's capital expenditure for another, but in general all the systems examined in detail are in the low-cost range.

A number of manufacturers produce LANs which function only with their own computer systems. These are not studied in detail as they are only of interest to those users who already have that manufacturer's equipment. They are listed, along with all LANs for which information is available, in Appendix A at the end of the book.

The book also examines the subject of standards for LANs. Those standards that are already published can be regarded as advisory rather than mandatory, and a manufacturer's product should not be disregarded solely because it deviates from some current or impending standard. With this in mind, the various standards are examined in detail, and their relevance to our area of interest i.e. low-cost LANs, discussed.

What are LANs?

Put simply, a LAN is a system of interconnection for computers and associated devices which allows interchange of information within a limited geographical area. I say 'simply' because despite the multi-syllable words used in the definition, nothing simpler will adequately cover the whole range of devices and systems which are currently grouped together under the heading 'LANs'. The term 'interchange of information' can cover transmission of voice, video, or digital signals in any direction between two or more devices and, as we shall see, the possibility of combining digital LANs with voice and video transmission systems is one that a number of manufacturers are considering. Likewise, 'computers and associated devices' and 'a limited geographical area' are both terms whose vagueness leaves a large number of possibilities open, suiting a field where examples from two extremes might hardly be recognised as the same type of thing.

However, bearing in mind the original definition, it is suitable in a number of ways to regard LANs as a product of converging technologies. As computers have simultaneously increased in power and become cheaper, the need has arisen for equally cheap and powerful ways of connecting them together and to their peripheral equipment, such as printers and disc stores, because a computer's effectiveness is determined by the information to which it can gain access, and the equipment it can control, as well as the intrinsic power of its processor.

The answer to the problem created by the need for multiple connections between computers and their peripherals was found in the communications bus. The bus is used in the internal structure of computers as a single communication highway to which all parts of the computer have access. Different types of information can travel along the same route but have different sources and destinations. This form of interconnection has distinct advantages over conventional point-to-point methods in terms of space and materials, and the falling cost of electronic components for the necessary control circuits means that this 'bus' concept is now a practical answer to networking needs.

In practice, the 'bus' systems used in real LANs are not immediately recognisable as such but they all do share one important factor i.e. they all have a transmission medium which is a shared resource.

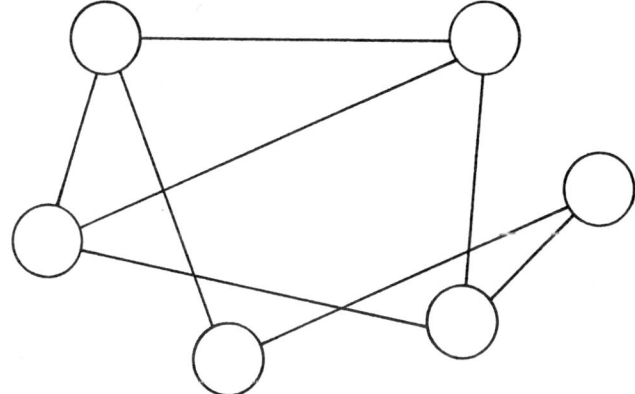

Normal interconnection

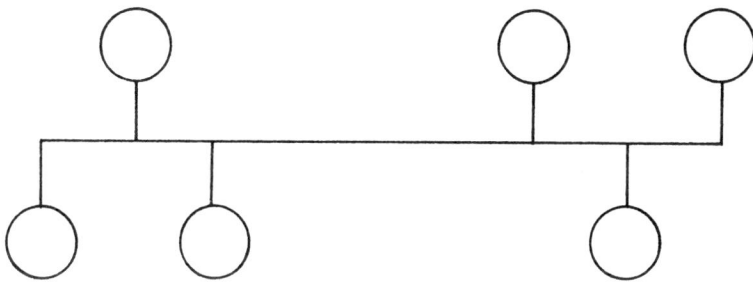

Bus interconnection

Fig. 1.1 Normal and bus interconnections

A communications network falls into the LAN category if it has most or all of the following characteristics:

1. All the devices on the network share the transmission medium i.e. the cable and/or controller.

2. The devices can operate independently of the network.

3. The area covered is small – usually less than one km. – and is confined to a single site e.g. office, factory, university campus.

4. The transmission rate for data is high compared with telecommunication networks, and transmission errors occur much less often.

5. Any device in the network can communicate with any other.

This list of conditions precludes the sort of data communication networks used in commerce and industry for transmitting information along telephone lines from site to site e.g. between banks. These are referred to as 'Wide Area Networks' (WANs) in order to distinguish them from LANs. In practice, a network may have characteristics from both types, so apply the definition loosely. It is worth remembering that a network of any description is only as useful as the use one makes of it, and that any item of equipment should fulfill a need – not just look impressive.

One other factor that LANs have in common is the relatively low cost of components, when compared with other types of network. WANs normally make use of the public telephone system, or leased lines, to transmit data and the charges for these lines can be a large and continuing part of the cost of the system, whereas most LANs just have initial installation expenses and cost little or nothing to run thereafter.

What does a LAN do?

Looking back to the original definition of a LAN in the previous section, this question can be answered by stating that a LAN allows 'interchange of information' between 'computer and associated devices'. Again, this doesn't really tell you a lot. A look at the types of equipment used with LANs and the sort of tasks a network carries out is much more informative. As well as mini– and micro-computers, LANs are commonly used to link:

    Keyboards, terminals, and visual display units.

    Printers and plotters.

    Mass storage units (hard disc and tape).

    Control equipment of various descriptions e.g. process control stations, computer-controlled machine tools, photo-typesetters.

    Facsimile equipment such as telecopiers.

    Virtually any piece of office equipment which has some form of computer connection.

LANs can also provide a connection to other networks, either through a computer which is attached to both networks, or through a dedicated device called a 'gateway'. Gateways can greatly expand the area covered by a LAN, particularly if they provide access to WANs or the public telecommunications system, and many of the manufacturers of LAN equipment include gateways to other standard systems in their product range.

In the field of office automation, LANs are allowing users to have access to central file storage and printing facilities whilst keeping the power of individual desktop personal computers. This allows the cost of expensive peripherals such as hard-disc storage systems and high-speed printers to be shared between a number of users. These two items are often referred to as 'file servers' and 'print servers' respectively. This makes sense when one views a single disc unit or printer as providing a service to the whole network.

Office automation is one of the main areas where LANs are making an impact, particularly for word processing tasks, but an equally promising area is the field of industrial control. Semi-intelligent monitoring and control stations in industrial process plants will adapt easily to networking and this will free any central process-control computer from the need to control a network as well as the plant itself. Automated workstations in manufacturing industries are also prime candidates for the application of LANs. Coordination of manufacturing processes can be achieved very efficiently where all workstations can communicate as desired, and adjust their activity in response to incoming information.

Who uses LANs?

At present, the number of organisations and individuals installing or operating LANs is small in comparison with the number using some sort of computing equipment. However, the benefits of LANs become apparent as the number of computers or workstations in an organisation increase. A few years ago, most small businesses had no computers at all and even medium-sized firms were usually on a single system. The explosion in personal computing since the mid-1970s has brought small, cheap computers within everyone's range and it is now unusual to find any reasonably-sized firm without a number of computers, either micro- or mini-based.

The proliferation within an organisation of often-incompatible computers and peripherals, and the duplication of resources this causes, mean that the introduction of a LAN can bring a number of benefits. As computer users seek to coordinate their expanding resources, more and more of them will be turning to some form of networking to solve their problems. With this in mind, the groups listed below are likely to be the main users and purchasers of LANs in the next decade.

1. Business organisations. Any firm or administrative organisation with a number of computers or associated devices will be able to use a LAN to connect these together, allowing the users to share electronic filing systems and printers. The installation of a LAN could also provide services such as electronic mail and memos, where incoming messages could be stored in an 'in-tray' in the computer's memory and printed out when the user next operates the device. The electronic or 'paperless' office concept currently being popularised by a number of office equipment manufacturers indicates that a number of other types of equipment could also be included in the network.

LANs in an office environment can thus be seen as a way of removing the need to physically transport or duplicate documents, with all the increased productivity and security that implies.

2. Research and development groups in science and engineering. Modern science and engineering research groups have taken to personal computers with enthusiasm. LANs will provide a means of combining the advantages of individual workstations and central databases. One common problem is the difficulty of transferring software and data from one system to another. If both are connected to the same LAN, this problem can be easily overcome. Experimental work involving the remote monitoring and control of equipment will also benefit from the flexibility that LANs can allow.

3. Industry. The possibilities of connecting automated process control and manufacturing equipment to networks for the purposes of monitoring and control by computers are receiving a great deal of attention from industry at the moment. The LAN is a prime candidate for the type of interconnection system required for most industrial environments, and the potential for growth in this field may well be greater than that in the more obvious field of office automation.

The application areas mentioned above are all ones where the increasing use of computer technology in an established field has stimulated the need for LANs or similar systems. However, computer technology itself has produced totally new areas of interest which have their own peculiar requirements. For example:

4. Education. Computing education has become part of the curriculum for schools and colleges with most having a large number of microcomputers available for student use. In order to control the use of these from a central point, where a teacher can examine and correct each student's work without leaving his own computer, the installation of some form of network is essential.

5. Home users. As home computing increases in popularity and power, it is possible that we may soon see the home computer user turning to simple LANs as a means of interconnection between his computers and peripherals. Modern electronics is allowing many people who were previously forced to work in an office to carry out the same tasks at home, blurring the distinction between the two.

A number of firms are encouraging their employees either to work at home using electronic aids or to set up their own businesses and sell their services to the parent company. These novel 'networking' approaches to business appear to be paying dividends for the firms and individuals involved but are only possible where a reliable data communication network is available.

Background information

A great deal of investigation has been carried out by various research organisations into the networking of computers over greater or lesser distances. Two of the most significant in their effect on commercial LAN design are the Cambridge Ring system, developed in the UK, and the Ethernet system, developed in the USA. Both of these are relevant to a general understanding of network techniques and will be discussed in detail in a later section. They are, in their original forms, high-speed, high-cost networks which are capable of a large number of functions. The commercial versions which have been developed from the original research networks are also relatively fast and expensive.

The advent of cheap computing power for everyone has produced a new and growing class of potential users for networks who share few of the concerns of the designers of the networks mentioned above. This new class of users, having acquired cheap computing, now require cheap interconnections with reliable equipment. The original research networks cannot provide this and so new LANs have been designed, which are based on the original principles, but which trade high speed and multiple functions for low cost and 'bundled' hardware and software. This last factor is one of the most important in the general acceptance of LAN technology today because whilst most research groups have the willingness and ability to modify the equipment they purchase, and to produce the necessary software, few commercial organisations will have either. The provision of all the hardware and software necessary for operating a LAN as a 'turnkey' system is vital to commercial acceptance. The software within the various computers allowing them to talk to the LAN intelligibly must also be included in such a package if it is to meet the requirements of most purchasers.

These factors will be dealt with more fully in the section on specifying and purchasing LANs but to summarise, the increasing availability of LAN technology has led away from the original types of system such as Ethernet and the Cambridge Ring which had these features:

> High data rates (typically up to 10 Mbits/sec.).

> Large numbers of possible connections to any type of device.

> Multiple functions in the LAN itself.

> Duplication of components for reliability.

> Little or no operating software – this must be supplied by the user.

And has led towards systems with wider commercial applicability and the following features:

> Reduced data rates (less than the big LANs by a factor of 10).

> Limited number of connections to specified types of device.

> Limited facilities, clearly defined by bundled operating software, built into the system hardware and installed with it.

LANs based on the Cambridge Ring or Ethernet systems will continue to gain popularity, particularly where they are adopted as standards (see the section on LAN standards) but for the small user the important question will not be 'How good is it?', but rather 'Will it do what I want at a price I can afford?'.

CHAPTER 2

Types of Local Area Network

Local Area Networks can be classified by broad types, where these types correspond to one or more of the characteristics of the system. LANs can be divided up in the following ways – by type of:

Topology; Access method; Signalling method; Transmission medium; Transmission mode.

Classification of networks by each of these characteristics allows certain types of comparison to be made but the relevance of each characteristic relates to the intended application.

Topology

To start with, let us consider the various forms of network topology, or interconnection pattern, as this normally gives some indication of the other network characteristics of a system. This is less true now than in the past as the recent proliferation of network technologies has led to a variety of systems similar in topology but otherwise very different. However, it is still true that certain topologies will contain certain other characteristics.

Star

The star network is developed from mainframe computer practice where a number of remote peripherals are connected on individual links to a central device, which performs all the logic and switching functions required of the system.

In this sense it is not a true LAN as the shared resource is represented by the central switching device rather than the transmission medium. It can be expanded so that each peripheral is itself the hub of a further star network.

Thus, addition of extra devices seems relatively straightforward either by adding to a peripheral cluster, or directly to the central device with an extra

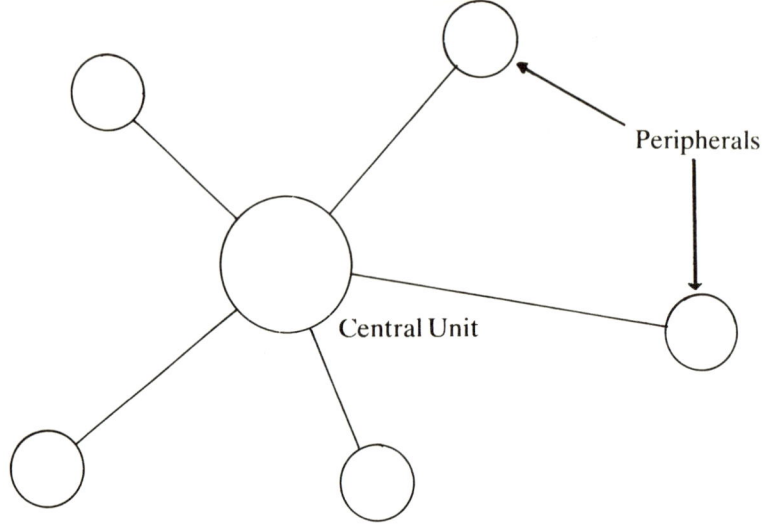

Fig. 2.1 Star Network

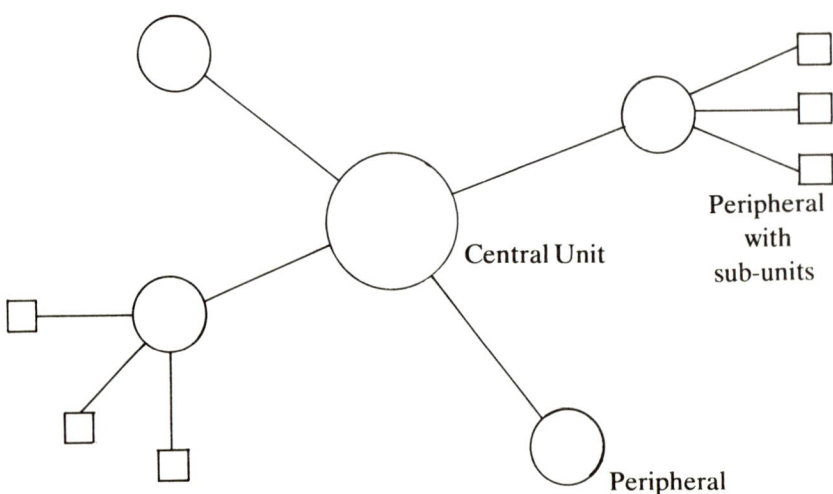

Fig. 2.2 Star of Stars Network

line. This, however, ignores the practical difficulties of running extra cables through existing installations, the problem caused by incompatible data transmission formats, and the necessity of having suitable hardware and software available at the central device. The importance of the star network to LAN technology lies in private telephone exchange systems (PABXs) which are already installed on most sites where a LAN would be suitable. A network based on the existing PABX would obviously have great advantages, particularly in installation costs. The difficulties of circuit-switched, rather than packet switched, systems and the limited data rates do not necessarily present insurmountable problems.

Loop

Again, this type of network layout is inherited from mainframe computer technology and is now of little importance. Basically it consists of a series of devices connected in a ring on a link which starts from and returns to the loop controller.

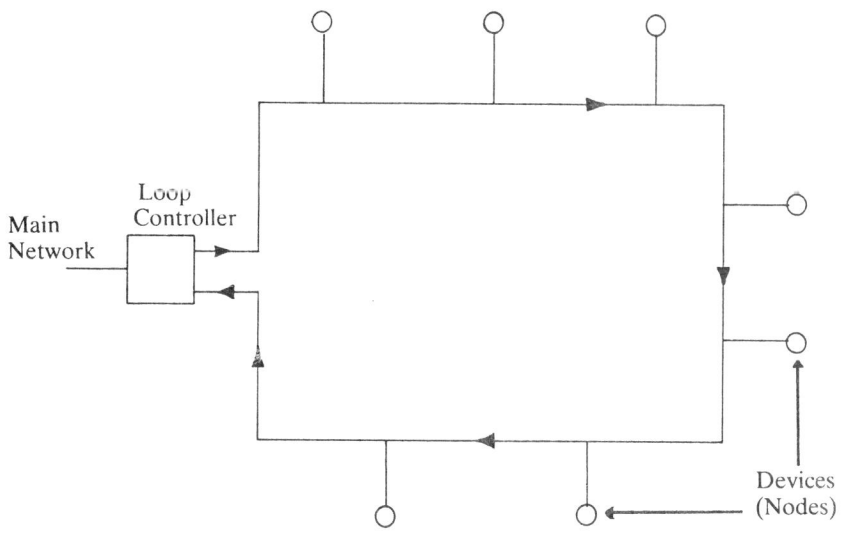

Fig. 2.3 Loop network

Data normally flows in one direction only and is passed from device to device until it reaches its destination. The loop controller decides which devices can send at any time and it is through the loop controller that data is transferred outside the loop. The method by which the controller operates the loop can vary. The functions switched to a loop are better served by ring or bus networks (see below).

Ring

A ring network is a closed loop containing all the devices on the network, and data flows sequentially from one device to the next.

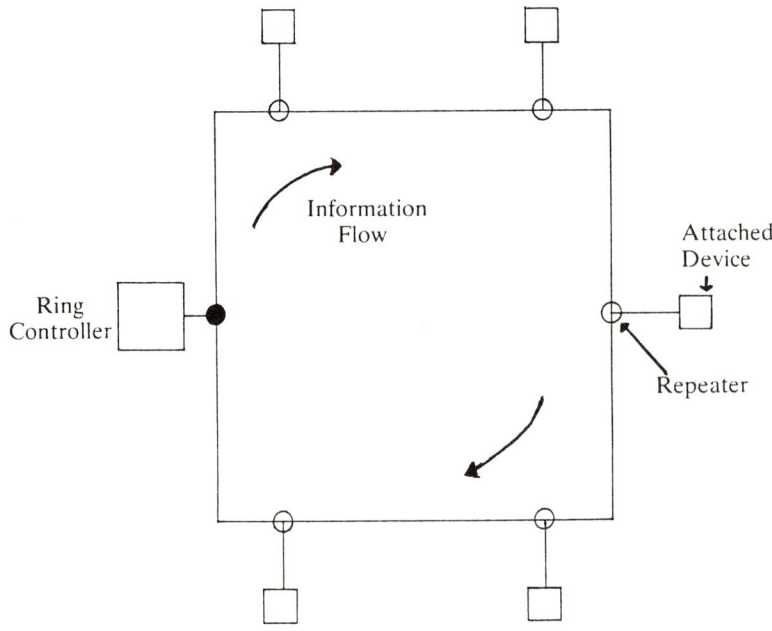

Fig. 2.4 Ring network

At each node in the ring, the transmitted information is received and retransmitted by a device called a *repeater*. The repeater also allows its attached device access to the ring and thus isolates the device from direct contact with the ring. This is necessary to avoid problems associated with the failure of an attached device, either due to power supply failure or damage.

In this case the repeater, which will be powered separately, continues to retransmit all information sent to it, regardless of whether the attached device is functioning. Repeaters are sometimes powered from the ring itself.

A second device is often employed at a node to interface the user device (e.g. terminal computer) to the repeater itself. This interface carries out buffering and ring access protocol functions, leaving the repeater free for reception and retransmission with the bare minimum of error checking. This allows the repeater to operate very rapidly.

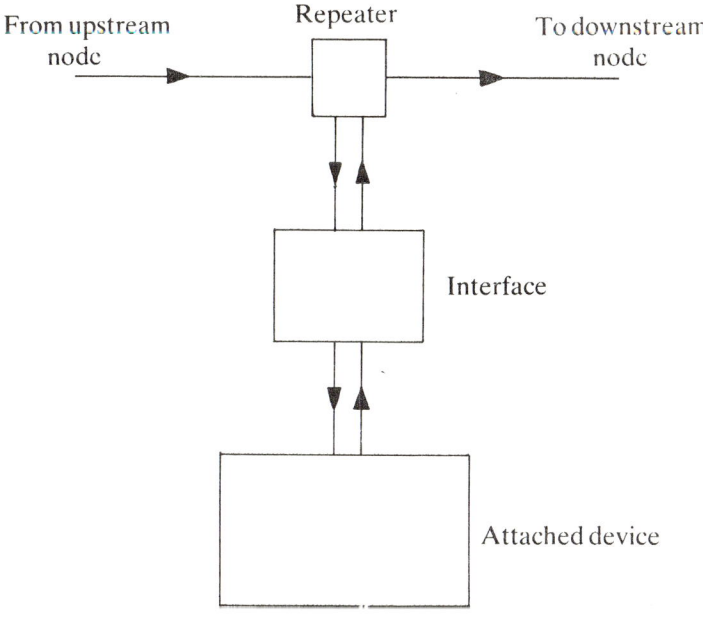

Fig. 2.5 Network node

If a node fails in a ring network, i.e. data is not received properly or not retransmitted, the system will also fail, unless some method of bypassing the failed node is available. This task can be accomplished in a number of ways: either by a simple relay switch, which removes the node from the system so that the link A-B-C becomes, on the failure of B, the direct link A-C; or by implementing some kind of switch back system, where a different ring is created on detection of a failed node (see diagram). This method is used in the Racal-Milgo Planet network, and ensures that a device will always be on the network as long as one of the devices on either side of it is still functioning. Note that this is not a dual ring in the true sense, as data is not transmitted in both directions under normal conditions.

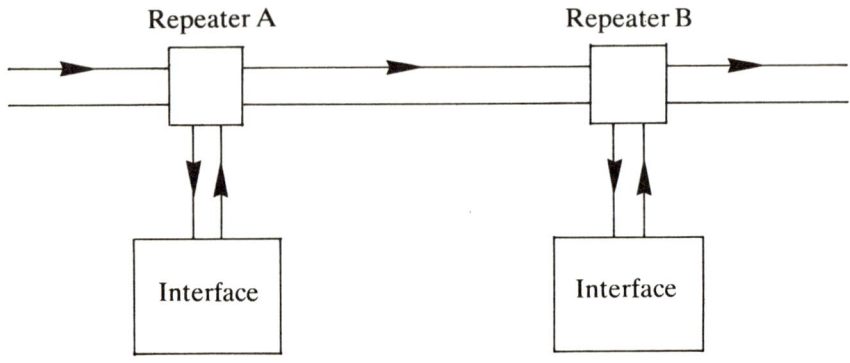

Fig. 2.6 Racal Milgo Planet Network

Rings normally have a monitor, or controller, device somewhere in the circuit, which is required to perform various tasks. It is not, as in the case of the loop network, concerned with controlling access. The ring is a true LAN and all nodes control their own access so the controller is involved with what might be termed the 'housekeeping' functions such as configuring the ring correctly when it is switched on, and removing any constantly-circulating packets of data, which may be the result of corruption during transmission, or failure of the transmitting or receiving node. Corruption during transmission may produce false transmit or receive addresses which will not be recognised by the network.

A ring network allows a variety of access methods and we will look at these in detail later. The main ones used are empty slot, buffer insertion and token passing. Similarly, the transmission medium varies greatly and all the possibilities will be examined in another section.

One disadvantage a ring system has in comparison with a bus, for example, is the relative difficulty in inserting new nodes into the network. To do this the ring must be broken and so data will be lost, or the ring will be rendered unusable until the new node is functioning. To avoid this, a duplication of loops as in the Planet system mentioned above, is necessary.

Bus

The bus network is based on the theory of interconnection developed in the internal architecture of computer systems, where the transmission medium between devices is a single shared resource, and the direction of transmission changes as required. This ensures that the minimum amount of material is used for interconnection.

The essential points of any bus system are that the system is open, i.e. there are no loops or circulating data streams, and that a signal produced at one node is transmitted to all nodes simultaneously before dying away. In this sense it can be likened to a radio broadcast system, with the broadcast restricted to the bus cable.

One of the greatest advantages of a bus network is that the transmission medium is passive, and all the power for the whole transmission is provided by the originating node. This means that all other devices are simply passive listeners and thus, the failure of one node does not affect the capacity of the rest of the network to transfer data. Also, the addition of extra nodes at any time will not cause the problems that would be associated with other types of network, making the bus an attractive proposition where the final number of nodes is undecided.

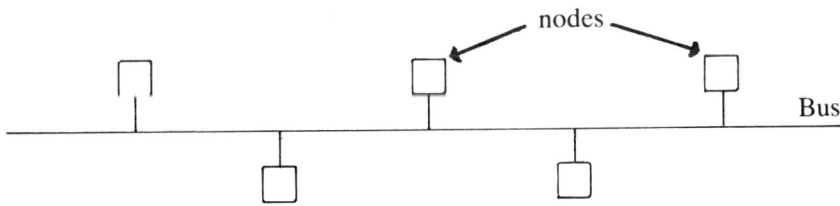

Fig. 2.7 Simple Bus Network

A bus system can be expanded and modified as necessary, without affecting its operation, unlike a ring where insertion of extra nodes can produce difficulties. Expansion may take the form of an extra length of bus, rather than just extra nodes, but this may require a repeating device to boost transmission to and from the additional bus. If this is done more than once the network now starts to look more like a star network, with the original length of bus acting as the central node.

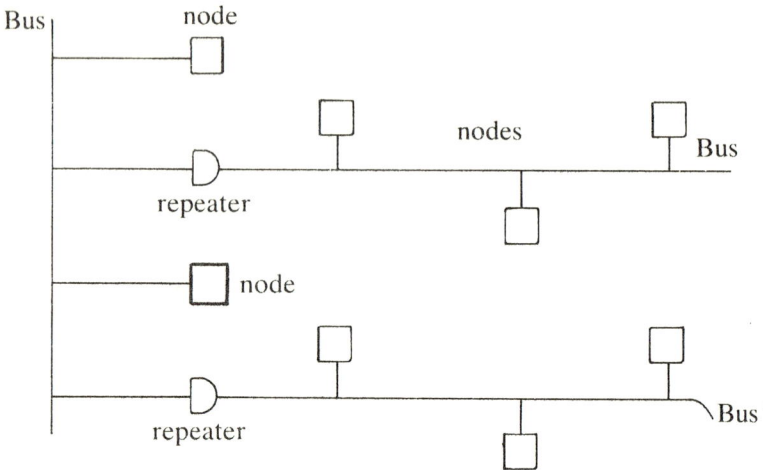

Fig. 2.8 Multiple bus network

Where passive branches are added, either to groups or individual nodes, the bus structure starts to look like a tree, and in fact this type of topology is often referred to as a tree network. However, it can essentially be considered, along with the bus-star network, as a form of bus, because it conforms to the bus characteristics listed above.

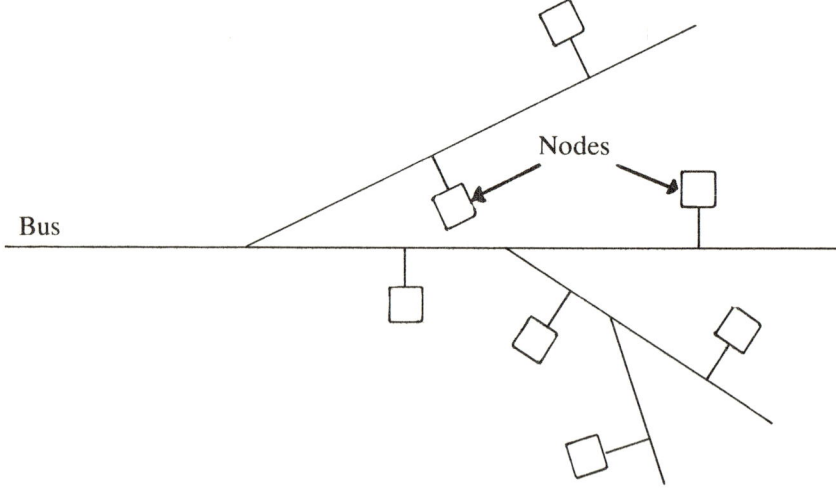

Fig. 2.9 Tree network

Bus networks come in two forms: baseband bus and broadband bus. The differences are important and, while baseband and broadband transmission of data is dealt with elsewhere, some discussion of the two types of bus is necessary here.

Essentially, in a baseband system, all nodes must contend for the use of the shared resource i.e. the bus. Only one device should transmit at a time, and to avoid the corruption of data caused by more than one device transmitting, some form of control must be exercised. Various sophisticated techniques have been developed to determine which device has priority and these are discussed in the section on access methods.

In a broadband system, the frequency spectrum available on the bus is subdivided into a number of sections, which can be allocated to the various nodes as required. Thus, each node can broadcast on its own frequency at any time, and contention problems are avoided. This would seem to be a theoretically much better solution to bus transmission problems but as we shall see, the practical difficulties of broadband bus networks are substantial.

Other topologies

Combinations of the forms discussed, and totally different ones, are possible but in practice, the bus and ring systems seem to be the basis for most commercially-available networks.

Access method

Where networks have a shared transmission medium i.e. in bus and ring networks, and their various subcategories, steps must be taken to ensure that all nodes can transmit data in an orderly manner. Broadband systems do this by allocation of a particular frequency band to each node, thus allowing unimpeded transmission. This method is a form of Frequency-Division Multiplexing (FDM) of the data carried by the network. FDM is dealt with in the section on broadband and baseband transmission.

Baseband networks allow each node to transmit by allocating each of them a period in which they can transmit freely. At the end of that period, access to the network for transmission is passed on to another node and the process is repeated. This is Time-Division Multiplexing (TDM), as the available time for transmission is divided up between the nodes.

The access methods or, more properly, the network-sharing techniques listed here are all forms of TDM and are relevant to baseband networks connected as a bus or ring. Only the ones relevant to current LAN design practice are covered in detail.

Bus-sharing techniques

The following access methods are all examples of bus-sharing techniques and are not necessarily compatible with ring networks. The main problem of a bus network is that of knowing when to transmit, as all devices have equal access rights to the same link. It can be solved in general either by contention, where the devices all vie for control, or by reservation, where the transmitting devices are allowed access in a pre-determined pattern. Contention effectively means that all devices have equal priority, whereas reservation implies that there is a fixed order of priority.

CSMA/CD

CSMA/CD stands for Carrier Sense Multiple Access, with Collision Detection. In a network employing this access method, all nodes listen constantly to the bus and only transmit if there is no transmission already on the bus. This is the Carrier Sense part of the name. If there is no transmission on the bus, any node with available data can transmit immediately, hence the term Multiple Access.

Should two or more nodes transmit simultaneously, the data on the bus will be distorted and all the nodes, which are still listening, will detect this. This Collision Detection will cause the relevant nodes to cease transmission and all other nodes will disregard what has already been sent. The transmitting nodes will then wait a random amount of time before trying to retransmit.

CSMA/CD is a development of CSMA which does not have the Collision Detection system. In this earlier method, packets of data which collided would continue to be transmitted until they ended, and an error would only be detected when an acknowledgment was not transmitted by the destination node. CSMA/CD thus improves the usability of a network over CSMA by the simple expedient of listening during, as well as before, transmission.

A variation on the theme is CSMA/CA, where CA stands for Collision Avoidance. In this network, nodes are allocated an individual time after the end of a transmission during which they can transmit. Where a device has no data, that time period is unused. If all devices do not transmit, system operation reverts to normal CSMA/CD until the next transmission. This is reckoned to be more efficient in utilisation of the bus than normal CSMA/CD but does require much more intelligence at each node to control allocation of time periods etc. It is however, suitable for networks where some nodes require much more access than others, or where time delays in the transmission of data from some nodes are critical.

CSMA/CD has a number of disadvantages – one is that the data packet minimum size is tied to the size of the network. Because the speed of transmission along the bus is finite, propagation delays along the bus mean that different nodes detect the same collision at different times. Thus the minimum packet size must be large enough for a collision to occur at all points in the system when two nodes transmit simultaneously. This requirement effectively limits the physical size of CSMA/CD buses as packet lengths over a certain size are impractical.

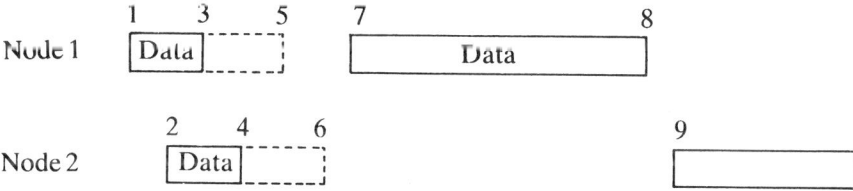

1   Node 1 starts transmitting.
2   Node 2 starts transmitting.
3-5 Node 1 detects collision, continues transmission to reinforce collision and then stops.
4-6 Node 2 detects collision, continues transmission to reinforce collision and then stops.
7   Node 1 retransmits after pause, finishes at 8.
9   Node 2 retransmits after longer pause.

Fig. 2.10 Packet collision in CSMA network

Another problem is that because of the random delay in transmitting after a collision, some devices may have to wait for an extended period to transmit data. As the bus becomes more heavily loaded, transmission delays will increase to an unacceptable level. This means that CSMA/CD is unsuitable for time-critical applications, such as real-time control, or voice transmission. It works best where a number of nodes have intermittent transmission requirements.

If data is destroyed or corrupted by some means other than collision, the transmitting device will not detect this. If, for example, the destination device has failed, this will only be discovered when the transmitter does not receive an acknowledgment within a certain time. Similarly, if the destination has received corrupted data, it must signal this fact to the transmitter and request a retransmission. CSMA/CD networks thus require a reasonable amount of intelligence at each node.

Token passing

Token passing is a method of bus reservation where a unique data packet is passed from node to node in the network. This packet is called a 'token' and possession of it allows a node to transmit data. No other devices can transmit while a node is in possession of the token, thus removing any possibility of collision of data. The token is passed on when the node has finished its transmission. The sequence of token passing is determined by the devices in the network and forms a logical 'ring' as the token passes through all the transmitting devices in the system and returns to its original node, after which it continues around the system.

Because this arrangement is a logical rather than physical one, devices can be included more than once in the sequence of transmission control or left out entirely. This allows weighting so that nodes with a greater transmission requirement have a proportionally greater time in control of the bus, and also allows listen-only devices to be excluded from control.

This weighting method has advantages over the random-access techniques of contention bus systems, such as CSMA/CD.

Token passing does, however, also have some problems. Failure of a node, for example, means the loss of the token and subsequent loss of bus control as the token will arrive at the failed node but never be passed on. The system must, therefore, have some provision for detecting node failure and then removing that node from the token-passing sequence when it is first included in the network.

These problems do not arise in contention bus networks and require some intelligence either distributed amongst the nodes, or concentrated in a bus monitor, to detect and overcome.

Ring access techniques

The following methods are ring access techniques and are primarily concerned with the various ways of inserting the data to be transmitted into a constant stream of data flowing around the ring. It is interesting to note that in a ring network, packets of data will circulate continuously unless physically removed from the ring, unlike the bus networks described above

Physical:

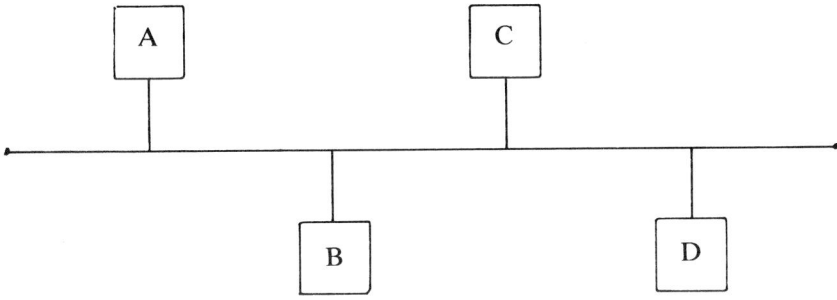

Logical:

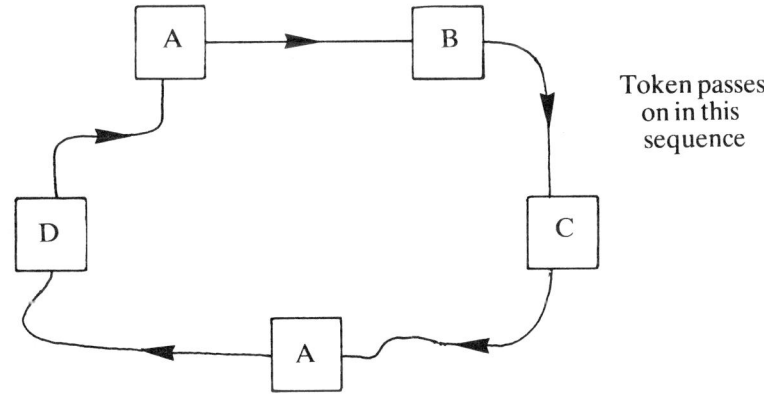

Fig. 2.11 Token-Passing network – physical and logical appearances

where data dies away after propagating to every point on the bus. This persistence of data requires that nodes remove as well as insert data constantly, as we shall see.

The currently popular ring access techniques are shown below.

Token passing

Token passing in a ring network is similar to its counterpart in a bus system. In one sense, all ring networks are forms of token-passing rings as the node desiring to transmit must be in possession of some item of data about the ring before it can take control.

However, the term is normally only applied in the case where a unique packet, recognisable by all nodes, is circulated by the ring. Any node ready to transmit when it encounters this token removes it from the ring and proceeds to transmit its data. At the end of transmission, the node relinquishes control and places the token back on the ring. The token then continues round the ring until the next node with data that is ready, receives the token and removes it from circulation.

Meanwhile, the transmitted data from the original node will proceed around the ring to its destination, where it will be received and buffered. It will then be sent back on to the network, with the addition of flags indicating conditions such as data received, data corrupted, etc. The original node will itself receive this packet and decide whether safe receipt is acknowledged, in which case the packet is removed from the ring, or retransmission is necessary, depending on the status of the packet.

The problems with token ring networks are similar to those of token bus networks, i.e. the loss of tokens due to corruption or device failure and the subsequent loss of transmission control. Most true ring systems have some kind of monitor station, as described earlier, and in a token ring, the monitor station must check for missing tokens or extra tokens, adjusting the ring as necessary to achieve correct operation.

Empty slot

Often referred to as the Cambridge Ring, although this term strictly refers to the type of empty slot system developed by the Computing Laboratory at Cambridge University, the empty slot access method employs one or more circulating packets or 'slots' in the ring to carry data. A slot is defined as 'empty' by the setting of a flag near the front end of the packet. Any device ready to transmit will examine the flag of an incoming packet as it passes around the ring and if it is found to be empty, the device will set the flag to indicate that the slot is now occupied, following which it will place its prepared data in the slot, to be sent around the ring.

The destination node recognises that the packet is for it by the internal address contained in the packet, and buffers the incoming data. It sets an indicator in the packet to say that data has been received and sends the packet back along the ring. At this stage the packet is still marked as full. When the original node receives back the packet it first transmitted, it removes it from the network by setting the empty/occupied flag to 'empty'. If the indicators in the packet show that the packet has been received in error, or not at all, the original node must wait for the next empty packet to arrive before it can retransmit the data. Nodes are not normally allowed to use the returned packets immediately as this would result in one node using

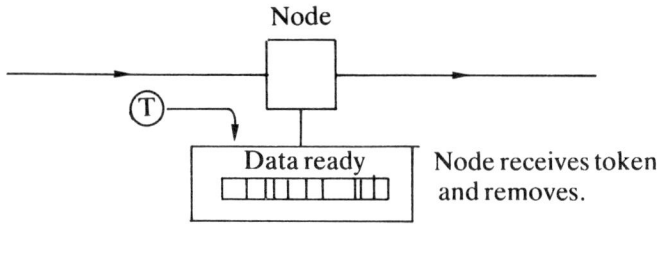

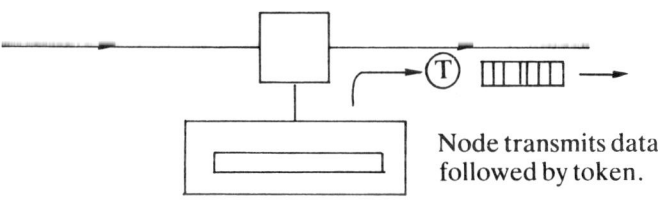

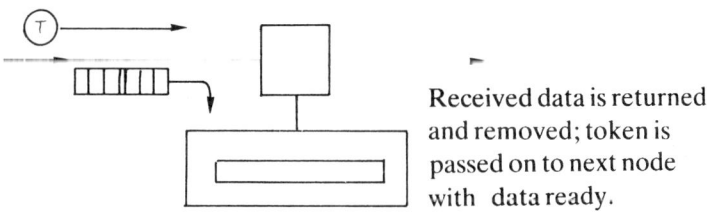

Fig. 2.12 Token Passing Operation

most or all of the ring capacity when it had data to transmit. Passing a recently-emptied packet to the next node allows all nodes to have equal access to the ring.

The empty slot can be regarded in some ways as a token since the node which receives it can then take control of the ring and transmit. Where only one slot is available to the ring users, control will pass around the ring in a fixed sequence and a time-division multiplexing of the system exists.

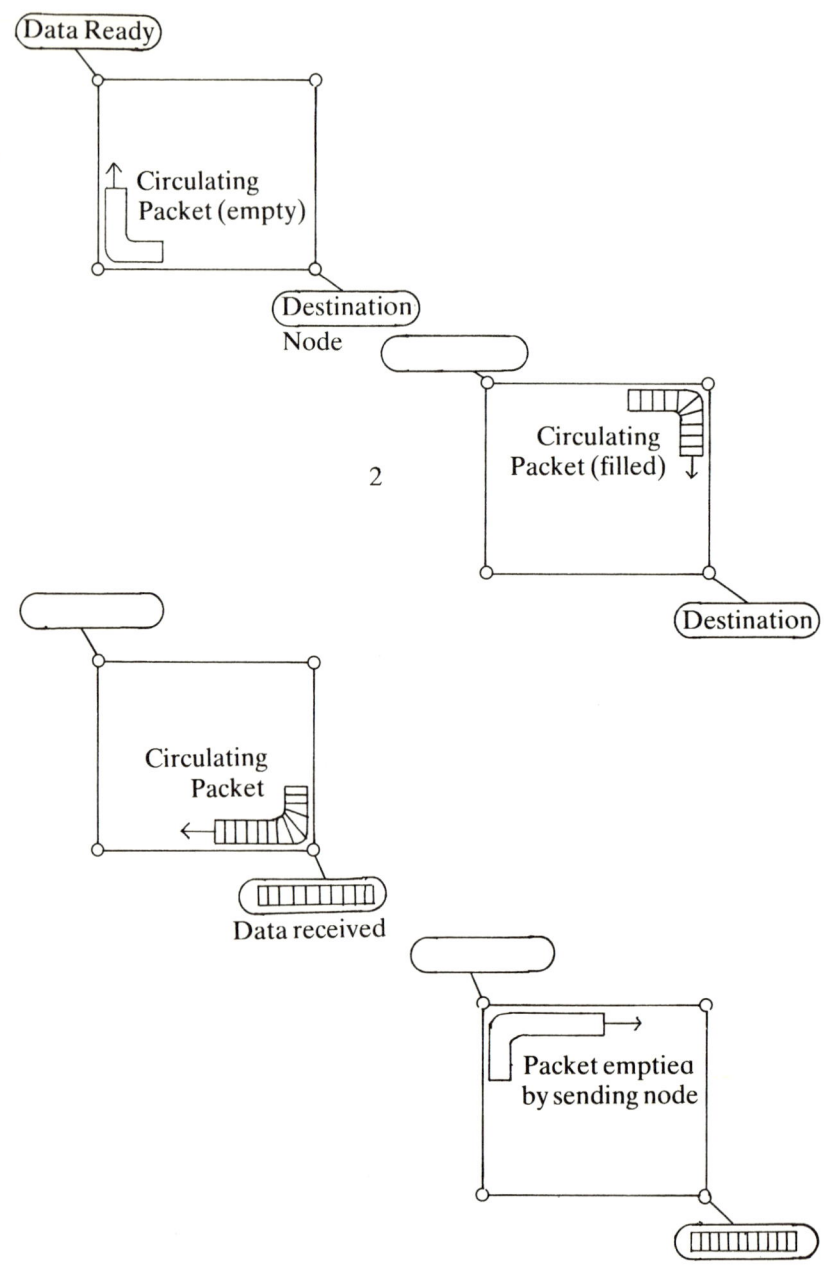

Fig. 2.13 Empty slot Operation

The packets in an empty slot ring are small and so to ensure proper transmission of streams of data, various protocols have to be observed at transmitter and receiver nodes to avoid buffer overflows, and to ensure that lost or damaged data is not ignored by the receiver.

The empty slot ring is easy to implement and can support high data transmission rates, typically 10 Mbits per second. Because it is a time-division multiplexed system like the other rings, data will always be transmitted within a short, defined period. This means that it is suitable for applications where data must be transmitted quickly, such as voice transmission or control systems. Increased loading on the ring increases all users' times between separate accesses equally, without going beyond a fixed maximum.

Error detection in an empty slot network is carried out both by the nodes, which check for such things as parity in packets, and by the monitor station, which is normally a part of such a ring system. The monitor station can identify continuously circulating packets by comparing each packet with what has gone before, and can thus remove packets which have not been removed by the nodes. It can also receive parity error messages from the nodes and thus identify the source of errors.

Buffer insertion

Buffer insertion, or register insertion, as it is sometimes known, is the other generally accepted technique for ring access.

Buffer insertion operates in the following manner: when a node has data to transmit, it senses the data being passed around the ring through its own repeater and on detection of the end of a packet, it switches the buffer containing the data for transmission into the ring circuit.

The data in the buffer is shifted serially out onto the ring and becomes part of the ring traffic, whilst incoming packets from the upstream nodes are shifted into the buffer and through it. In this way the buffer itself becomes part of the ring and the ring increases in size by the length of the buffer.

As in other ring systems, the outgoing packet of data travels to its destination node and then on, round the ring, until it arrives back at its origin. Once it again fills the buffer, which is still part of the ring circuit, and the node detects its return, the buffer is removed from the ring circuit and the ring reduces to its previous size.

Buffer insertion allows larger packet sizes than empty slot rings, within limits. The buffer size defines the packet size and this is limited by the hardware costs of producing a large buffer at each node.

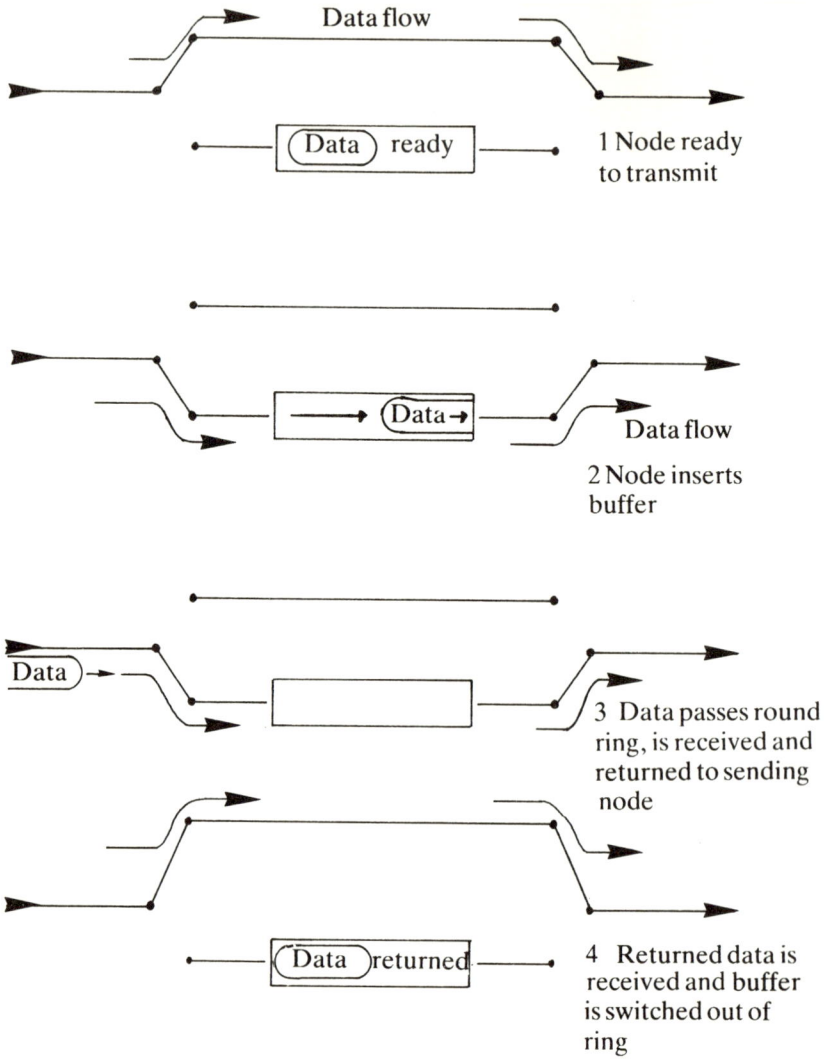

Fig. 2.14 Buffer insertion operation

Because the size of the ring varies with the number of nodes inserting data, transmission time, as opposed to time waiting to transmit, is a variable, and this together with the hardware problems associated with large buffers, limit the size to which a buffer insertion ring can grow.

Signalling method

Data must be transmitted through the network in a coherent manner and reach its destination unimpaired. To do this, signalling techniques have evolved which fall into two distinct categories, which can be described simply as baseband and broadband signalling methods.

The two terms indicate whether the data is used to modulate a carrier signal (as in radio transmissions) or not.

The methods are described below.

Baseband transmission

Baseband transmission systems are those where the data for transmission is introduced directly to the transmission medium, without any form of modulation. The bandwidth of the system is therefore that of the original data stream, i.e. from 0 Hz upwards.

Baseband transmitters and receivers (transceivers) are thus very simple to construct and their simplicity and low cost have made baseband local area networks very popular. In its simplest form, baseband data is transmitted as a stream of binary 1s and 0s, represented by voltage levels or light pulses, depending on the transmission medium.

Baseband systems do suffer from a number of drawbacks, the most significant of these being the fact that only one transmitter can occupy the network at any time. Whilst one node of a network is talking, all others in the system are required to keep silent and listen.

This leads to a network whose normal data rate is much higher than the average data rate of the devices attached to it, because it effectively multiplexes the transmitted signals from each node in time (This is known as Time Division Multiplexing, or TDM).

The data rate of a baseband system must, therefore, be greater than the product of the average data rate of the attached transmitters and the number of transmitters, otherwise there is a danger of data being lost. e.g. in a system with 10 nodes, all transmitting at 10 kilobits per second, the network data rate must be greater than 10x10000 i.e. greater than 100 kilobits per second.

This requirement for high frequency transmission leads to use of high-bandwidth cables in order to reduce the effects of attenuation and distortion on the high-speed digital signals.

Both high frequency and distance have distorting effects on data transmission and so baseband networks tend to cover short distances where high data rates are required. Some systems designed to cover larger areas require 'repeaters' which reconstitute and boost the signal at regular intervals e.g. Ethernet.

Synchronisation of data in baseband systems is also a problem, as a long stream of 1s or 0s will seem like an unchanging signal. This can be countered by transmitting a separate synchronisation signal but this is not possible in networks which only have a single connection between nodes.

Alternatively, the data can be encoded in some way so that it synchronises itself. There are various methods for doing this and the most popular currently is 'Manchester Encoding (ref)'. See *Glossary of Terms* for detailed explanation.

Broadband transmission

Broadband transmission systems utilise the information signal to modulate a carrier wave of fixed frequency. This carrier is propagated along the network and demodulated at the receiver to reconstitute the original information signal. As the carrier can, in theory, have any frequency, the method is called broadband transmission.

The technology for this method has been developed from cable television methods, where a number of information signals must be carried along a single connector. This system, generally referred to as CATV (Community Antenna TV), operates by frequency-multiplexing a number of information signals onto one connection. The various signals are, therefore, not distinguished by separation in time (TDM, as discussed in the section on baseband), but by the difference between the various carrier wave frequencies used. With a bandwidth of up to 300MHz, CATV systems allow a substantial number of digital transmissions to be frequency-division multiplexed on a single cable.

The available bandwidth is normally split into distinct groups. For example, all transmission channels will be grouped together in a single frequency band, and reception channels will be kept separate in another band. This concept can be taken further and individual devices can be assigned unique frequency bands for their own use.

Some broadband LANs, such as the WANG system assign different frequency bands for the different types of transmission e.g. one band for digital data, one for voice, one for video, etc. This highlights one of the great advantages of broadband systems, which is the ability to handle all kinds of information, including colour video transmissions. Baseband systems cannot compete in this respect.

The important device in a broadband system is the radio frequency transmitter and receiver. Every node in the network must have one in order to modulate its transmissions and demodulate its received data. These devices are normally referred to as RF modems (for Radio Frequency MOdulator and DEModulator) and the cost of these is often a limiting factor in the use of broadband networks, particularly as carrier frequency and data rate increase.

However, much of the other equipment required for a broadband network is already available and produced in large quantities for CATV applications, thus bringing the benefits of scale to reducing installation costs in this area.

Broadband transmission systems consist of one or two cables and work as described below.

Where the network is a 2-cable system, one cable is used for data transmission and the other for data reception (see diagram).

2-Cable system

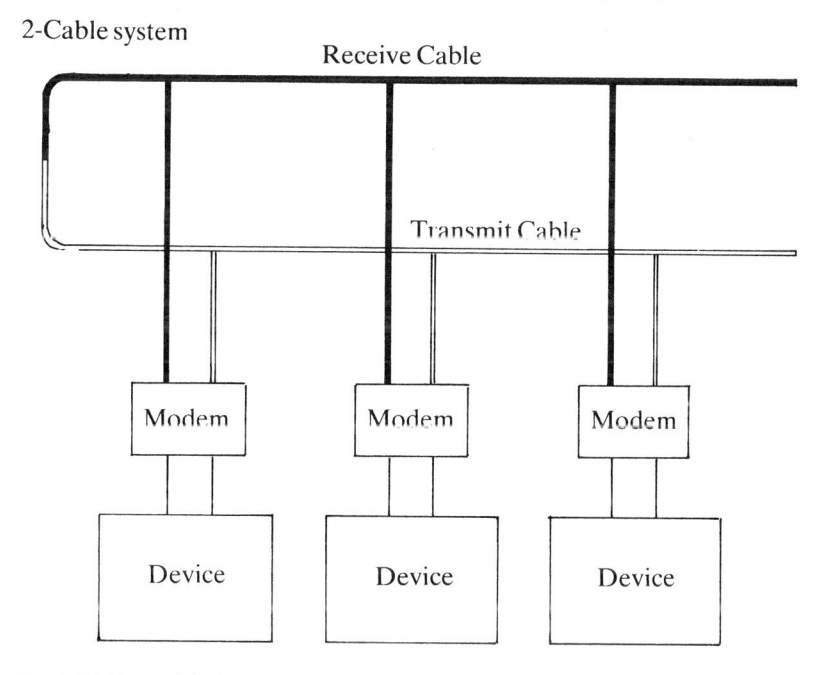

Fig. 2.15 Two-cable broadband network. Typical sub-division of frequency bands in a commercial broadband network

To ensure that data is transferred from the transmit cable to the receive cable, they must be looped together at one end, either directly (a passive connection) or through an amplifying unit generally referred to as a 'headend' (an active connection). This method of transmitting on one cable and receiving on another allows much of the standard CATV equipment, which is designed for unidirectional transmission (i.e. from antenna to receiver) to be used directly.

Single-cable systems must split the system bandwidth in order to separate transmit and receive bands. The bandwidth is normally split in the middle with all transmissions on one side of the centre frequency, and all received signals on the other. This obviously requires an active device as a headend, in order to transpose the frequencies of the transmitted signals into the receive band.

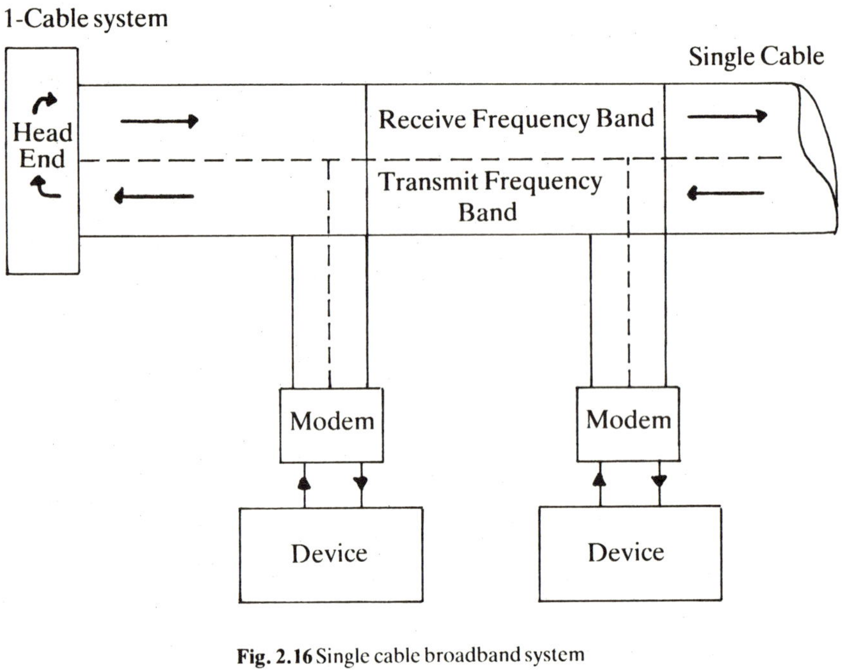

1-Cable system

Fig. 2.16 Single cable broadband system

The examples given above have assumed only one transmit and/or receive frequency — this is obviously not the way to utilise the full potential of a broadband system. Communication will be limited to an interchange between two devices with the correct modem frequency and connection to further devices will require extra modems to be attached to each device.

The transmit and receive bands are, therefore, each split up into a number of frequencies, each of which can be used as a transmission channel. We now have the potential for a number of simultaneous transmissions, but each will still be between the two devices with the correct modem frequencies.

Two methods are used to avoid the restrictions which exist, particularly in systems which have a number of ports onto a network e.g. mainframe computers. These types of device still need a modem per channel unless one of the following strategies is adopted.

A single frequency can be time-division multiplexed in the manner discussed for baseband networks thus allowing a single modem to be used for data transmission to and from a number of devices. The devices would be identified by an address contained in each packet of data.

Alternatively, each node in the network can be equipped with what is termed a Frequency-Agile Modem or FAM. This type of modem can alter its transmit and receive frequencies on demand, making interconnection to any other node possible on any frequency.

Two devices which must communicate, therefore, only need to decide on a pair of suitable frequencies to ensure a connection for the duration of the transmission. In practice, a node requiring access to the network must request a channel from some sort of controller, normally in the headend, which will allocate transmit and receive nodes to operate on these channels.

This method requires some sophisticated controls, and frequency-agile modems are not cheap, but represents the best utilisation of broadband networks. Channels will stand idle only for short periods, and will not depend on individual nodes for use.

In contrast, data rates can be kept low, which is advantageous, because when a channel is allocated, there is no time-multiplexing of data.

Transmission medium

The transmission medium is the physical connection between nodes in the network. We shall only look at those types of transmission medium which are currently in use in proprietary local area networks, and avoid the proposed or possible alternatives, in order to keep a simple viewpoint. For example, we will not consider radio or direct laser transmission as these are not used except in one-off systems and research networks, e.g. the ALOHA network at the University of Hawaii (see Chapter 7)

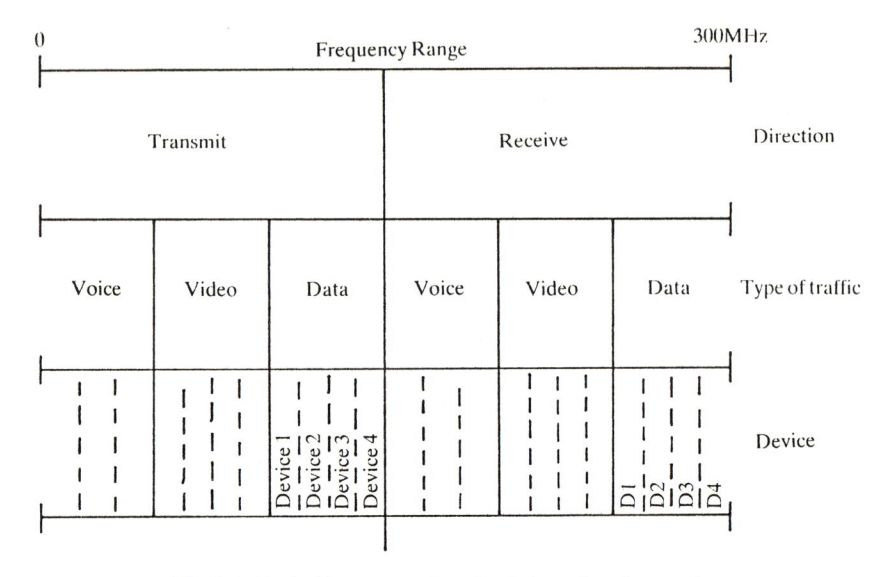

Fig. 2.17 Typical frequency allocation in broadband network

The transmission media of importance in current networks are various forms of electrical conductors, which are generally popular, and fibre optics, which are not so widespread. There are three main types of electrical conductor in common use and these are indicated below:

Twisted pair

The twisted pair is a pair of single insulated conductors twisted together for the purposes of minimising noise pickup from the environment. Twisted pairs are a development of telephony and have been used for many years to carry analogue voice traffic in telephone networks. The fact that they are already installed in many buildings as a provision for extra telephones can be considered an advantage.

Fig. 2.18 Twisted pair cable

Because of their long history and wide usage, twisted pair connections are cheap, widely available, and simple to install. The technology of the driver and receiver devices is well established and in general, this method of transmission can seem very attractive.

However, it does have a number of disadvantages. Because it is designed for analogue voice transmissions, it cannot support high data rates over long distances. The conductors have a high capacitance and high frequency signals are degraded in quality very quickly. Thus repeaters are needed at regular intervals if high data rates are required.

Twisted pairs also radiate a considerable amount of energy, whilst being susceptible to outside noise. This may be a considerable problem in areas containing other electrically sensitive equipment, or where security of communication is important.

Ribbon/multicore cables

These two types can be regarded as one for the purposes of this discussion, as they exhibit the same basic strengths and weaknesses.

The greatest advantage is that the provision of a number of separate conductors allows the separation of control, data and synchronisation signals within the transmitted signal. This in turn serves to reduce the complexity, and therefore cost, of the network interfaces at each node so although the cost of the cable may be greater than other methods, the cost per node is less.

The main problem with ribbon and multicore cables is that, like twisted pairs, they have a high capacitance per metre and thus a high attenuation. This severely restricts the data rate if repeaters are not used. However, the provision of more than one conductor in parallel in the connection means that the true data rate of the link can be much greater than the data rate for a single conductor in the link. In effect, the true data rate will be the data rate of a single conductor multiplied by the number of parallel data conductors.

Ribbon/multicore connections have had some success because of the relative simplicity of attached hardware and opportunity for improving data rates. They are used, for example, in Zynar's Net/One LAN, which has proved popular. However, most of the new networks appearing on the market use the third form of electrical transmission medium, coaxial cable.

Coaxial cable

Coaxial cable consists of a central conductor surrounded by insulating dielectric material and covered with a conducting screen which forms the signal return path. The cable has a protective insulating sheath on the outside (see diagram).

The cable itself comes in a variety of types, which differ in the materials used to form the various layers. In the coaxial cable used for CATV (and thus broadband LAN) applications, the cable screen consists of a seamless extruded aluminium tube which makes the cable both strong and stiff. It has a characteristic impedance of 75 ohm. In contrast, baseband coaxial cable has a copper mesh screen and a characteristic impedance of 50 ohm, making it more flexible but also more susceptible to damage.

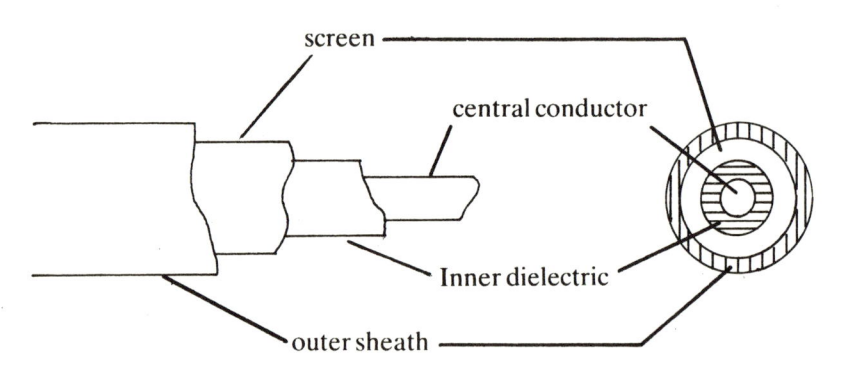

Fig. 2.19 Coaxial cable

Coaxial cable has a relatively good high-frequency response due to its low capacitance and its overall screen gives good noise immunity. The cost varies according to the type being used.

In general, coaxial cable for broadband systems will be more expensive than cable for baseband use. This may prove to be a significant disadvantage in certain types of installation.

Fibre optics

Fibre optic transmission has much greater potential in local area networks, with a large number of advantages over electrical methods as we shall see. However, a number of practical difficulties must be overcome before it finds widespread acceptance.

Fibre optics' main radical difference from the methods of transmission already discussed is that it conducts light rather than electricity. This is at the same time its strength and its weakness.

A fibre optic cable consists of a light-conducting core surrounded by another material – the cladding. The cable is normally made from glass or plastic and the cladding part has a different refractive index from the core, which minimizes light loss through the sides of the cable and promotes internal reflections down the length of the core.

The technology of the material has advanced to the stage where fibre optics are much thinner and cheaper to produce than the equivalent electrical conductor. They also have a much lower attentuation which will allow connections over a greater distance before a repeater is necessary to boost the signal.

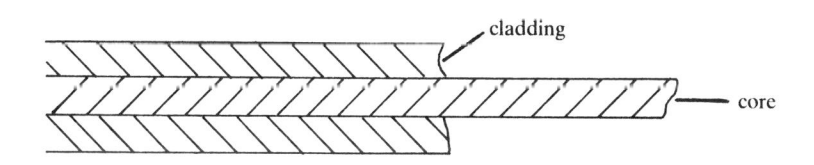

Fig. 2.20 Fibre Optic

Bandwidth of a fibre optic transmission system is typically much greater than electrical cables, which makes it suitable for all broadband and high-speed baseband networks. However, the non-electrical nature of the transmitted signal produces some difficulties. The most significant is the necessity of converting the signal from an electrical one to an optical one on transmission and reversing on reception.

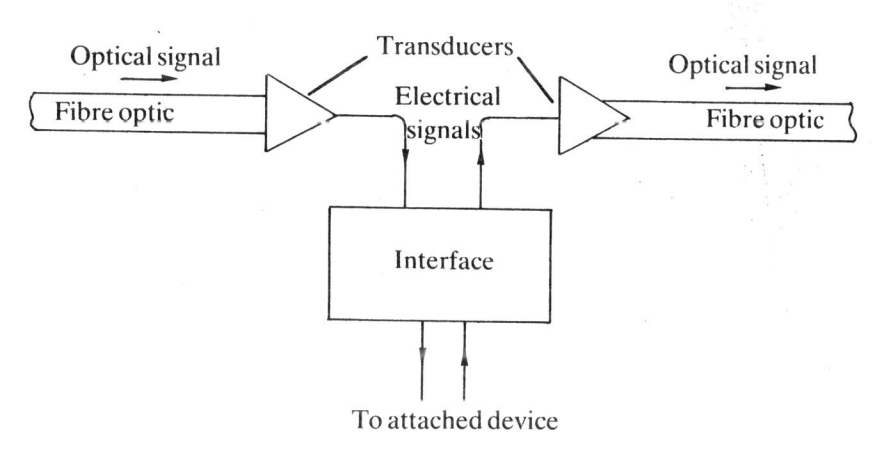

Fig. 2.21 Fibre optic node

The amount of hardware required at each node is thus greater than it might be in an equivalent electrical system, and the fact that these devices must be produced specially for this purpose means that they are not yet available cheaply.

Also the practical difficulties of installing a receiver and a transmitter at both ends of a fibre optic cable mean that it is essentially a one-way medium. This limits its use to ring networks or similar, unless a second cable is used.

Fibre optics are, of course, completely immune to all forms of electrical noise pickup. This alone makes them very attractive for use in electrically noisy environments such as factories. They cannot be tapped or interfered with in the same way as electrical connections and so are also suitable for networks where security is important.

It seems probable that despite the disadvantages listed, fibre optic connections will gradually become more popular, particularly as they are increasingly used in telecommunications installations.

Transmission mode

A quick examination of the type of transmission mode used is probably helpful although, in practice, the transmission mode is usually determined by other factors in the network.

Transmission mode is really a description of the way data is organised for transmission from one node to another in the network and divides into three general groups with the following headings:

   Circuit-switched
   Message-switched
   Packet-switched

The differences are contained within the titles. Circuit-switched networks are ones which dedicate a complete physical connection i.e. an electrical circuit, centralised switching facility. A telephone system with a central exchange is a good example of a circuit-switched network.

Message-switched are ones which only allow a single pair of nodes to have access to the transmission medium for the duration of their conversation. The practical drawbacks of this type of transmission mode when used in anything other than a star network are immediately obvious – any other pair of devices wishing to converse may suffer an unacceptable time delay before they gain access to the network.

Packet-switched networks allow a transmitting node access to the transmission medium for the time required to send an arbitrary amount of data. The amount of data in this 'packet' can be set to suit the operating conditions of the network. Too little data will result in a waste of the network's resources as an unnecessary amount of control information e.g. destination address, error-checking codes, will be sent with each packet. Too much data in a packet will result in long access times for nodes wishing to transmit, which is equally undesirable.

Most currently-available LANs use packet switching as their transmission mode, even where a star configuration is used, and it is safe to assume that they will continue to do so.

CHAPTER 3

Standards

The standards referred to in this chapter are those concerned with the behaviour of LANs. That is, the rules and regulations governing the physical design of a LAN and the rules, or protocols, which control the data flow in the LAN.

The various standards currently in force are more or less comprehensive but must be regarded as advisory, and their variations mean that adhering to one may prevent the others from being used.

What use are standards?

What use are standards? The immediate answer to this question is that standardisation of equipment in any field will normally bring benefits to the end user or consumer by allowing the manufacturers to produce items of equipment which are compatible with one another and are, therefore, more versatile and thus more cost-effective. If all manufacturers adhere to standards for interconnection, they will be producing similar items, and thus the component parts will be the same, which should reduce costs to the manufacturers. This saving will hopefully be passed on to the consumer.

Some sort of general agreement on function is obviously necessary if different items of equipment are to work together successfully but it is still a debatable point that LAN technology has 'matured' sufficiently to benefit from a single rigid specification. In other words, many people in the field believe that there is still work to be done, in research and development, before the best solution for everyone's needs is apparent.

Even this 'wait and see' attitude ignores the fact that potential LAN users are far from being a homogenous group with identical requirements. For example, the overriding requirement for most office automation networks would be efficient utilisation of network equipment, keeping the cost per node as low as possible. In contrast, process control network users would see guaranteed access with minimum delay as the most important requirement. A standard designed for one of these requirements may not necessarily be suitable for the other.

In practice, proposed standards have emerged in the wake of successful systems and so in general the standard conforms to something the user already has, rather than vice-versa.

This pattern of the rules coming after the activity is one that often occurs in a fast-developing field such as telecommunications or computing, where the organisations which define the rules are not themselves the innovators. It is obviously impractical for a standards organisation to sanction one set of standards if a large number of users have already decided to work with another set and so standards are very much a consensus decision.

In the past, when local area networks were few and far between, they were designed as one-off systems and no emphasis was placed on compatibility or standardisation. As long as the system fulfilled its requirements, it was perfectly acceptable.

Now, with a huge increase in the number of users and potential users, and the proliferation of manufacturers and suppliers, it is becoming apparent that a certain amount of standardisation is necessary. This will allow users to put together a working LAN from various manufacturers' components and thus allow them to take advantage of particular features of each type of equipment. This 'kit' approach to system design has long been the norm in mini- and micro- computing where widely-accepted interconnection standards such as RS232C, 20mA loop, and IEEE488 have minimised (although not removed completely) the difficulties of interconnection between different types of equipment.

Standards

The following section will give some information about the currently-accepted standards. The various sets of standards are sometimes contradictory and sometimes complementary, and the points of contention will be indicated. The pre-eminent system for interconnection is the Open System Interconnection (OSI) model proposed by the International Standards Organisation (ISO).

Open system interconnections

Open system interconnection is a model proposed by the ISO for information interchange between computers and peripherals. It is an idealised system which is meant to cover all types of connection, not just LANs, and it consists of a seven-layer architecture of protocols for enabling two devices to talk together (see Fig. 3.1).

These seven layers are not physical devices, but rather sets of rules controlling the actions of the interconnection hardware and software at various levels.

OSI is an attempt to define a single consistent set of rules which, if followed, will allow any computer or peripheral to talk to any other. It applies to the whole computer field and LANs are only a small part of its scope.

OSI is of great interest to manufacturers who produce a range of equipment or find that their equipment is connected to a variety of other devices, because it will ensure that everything will work together correctly without any adjustments.

So far, LAN suppliers are only bringing their products into line with the lower layers of the 7-layer model (if at all) and while it is likely that some, though not all, LANs will eventually conform to the ISO model, the present situation is encouraging a 'wait-and-see' attitude.

The OSI reference model (Fig.3.1) indicates the way groups of functions within the system are organised. Each layer appears to communicate directly with the equivalent layer at the other end of the communications link, which requires the layers below it to be 'transparent' when viewed from above. This modularisation of the protocols and functions allows changes to be made at any level without affecting other layers, which should still see the same conditions after any modification.

The layers are split as follows:

1. Physical medium: This exists below the seven defined layers and represents the hardware which carries the data from one point to another in the network. This could normally consist of the electrical or fibre-optic cable and its associated drivers and receivers.

2. Physical layer – 1: This layer provides and controls the physical connections between two devices in a network i.e. it controls the transfer of data bits along the physical medium, and the associated hardware.

3. Data link layer – 2: The data link layer provides control for reliable transfer of blocks between adjacent systems. It supervises error detection and recovery.

4. Network layer – 3: The network layer handles the forwarding of the data from adjacent systems on to their final destinations. It allows the equipment in the network to act as a relay station if the incoming data is bound for another place.

5. Transport layer – 4: This layer is concerned with end-to-end control of the transportation of data, and the optimisation of use of network resources.

6. Session layer – 5: The session layer is concerned with dialogue control and synchronisation, initialisation and support of recovery of distributed processing. In other words, it supervises the setting up, conduct, and termination of a conversation or 'session' between two devices in the network.

7. Presentation layer – 6: The presentation layer is concerned with fixing data formats, codes and data representation in the network device. It supervises the way information is presented to the application program using the network.

8. Application layer – 7: This is the highest layer in the model and the one that communicates directly with the user's application program. Its rules and protocols are concerned with the requirements of the applications program.

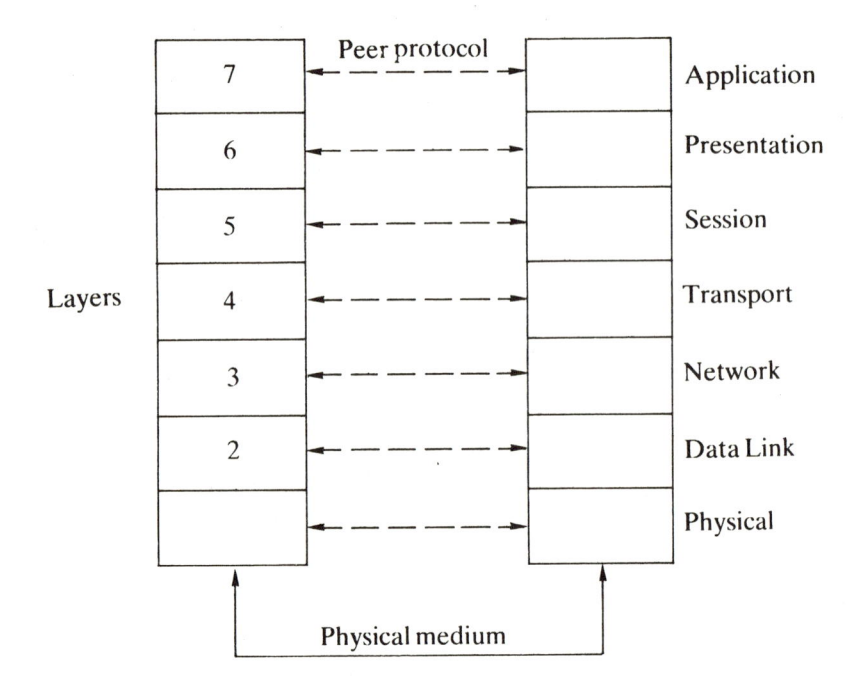

Fig. 3.1 ISO 7 layer model

There is a great deal of information available about OSI and so it is unnecessary to go into any more detail about it here. Its aims are highly laudable but much of the literature on the subject is so abstruse and impenetrable that it seems to have little immediate relevance to the practical problems involved in getting devices to talk usefully to one another. At the moment, the important thing about OSI is to be aware that it exists, and that LAN manufacturers will be incorporating some or all of its concepts in their products if they desire them to be universally applicable.

The question of universal applicability is going to be most important to the large systems manufacturers who also supply computing or telecommunications equipment, as they will need products compatible with a wide range of systems. For example, the Ethernet consortium (consisting of Xerox, Digital Equipment Corporation, Intel and others) have brought their Ethernet specifications into line with the lower layers of OSI.

The smaller manufacturers, selling to narrow markets, or concentrating on low-cost systems, will be less concerned with OSI compatibility. Their products are likely to conform to OSI only insofar as this does not interfere with their most important characteristics which are likely to be:

1. Suitability for a particular application.
2. Low cost.

Meanwhile, the ISO is doing further work on specific LAN standards which should soon emerge to give international leadership in the direction of LAN development.

IEEE 802

The American Institute of Electrical and Electronic Engineers (IEEE) is the main body in the USA concerned with standards for the electrical and computing industries. Conscious of a need for standards in the developing LAN field, it constituted a committee to produce them. The committee's number, 802, has been given to the standards it has presented.

The 802 committee has been working on LAN standards since 1980 and the work it has produced is generally regarded as the nearest to a comprehensive set of standards yet available.

The standards work was divided up among a number of subcommittees, each responsible for a particular aspect of LAN definition. It soon became apparent that the various special interest groups represented on the subcommittees wanted different things from a LAN and so, in order to

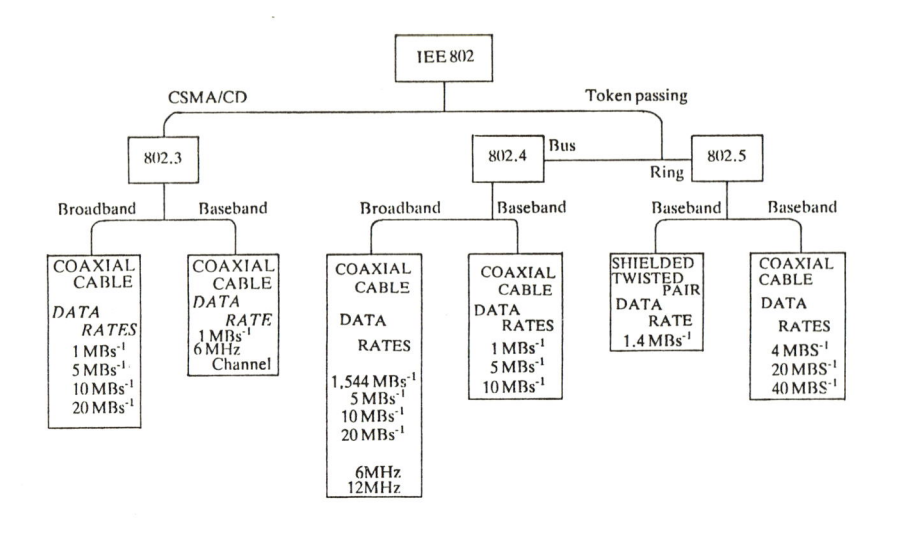

```
                                IEE 802
           CSMA/CD                            Token passing
       ┌──────┴──────┐              ┌──────────┴──────────┐
     802.3                        802.4  Bus            802.5
                                         Ring
   ┌────┴────┐                  ┌────────┴────────┐   ┌────┴────┐
Broadband  Baseband          Broadband        Baseband Baseband Baseband
```

Fig. 3.2 IEEE 802 Committee proposals

802.3 Broadband — COAXIAL CABLE
DATA RATES
1 MBs^{-1}
5 MBs^{-1}
10 MBs^{-1}
20 MBs^{-1}

802.3 Baseband — COAXIAL CABLE
DATA RATE
1 MBs^{-1}
6 MHz Channel

802.4 Broadband — COAXIAL CABLE
DATA RATES
1,544 MBs^{-1}
5 MBs^{-1}
10 MBs^{-1}
20 MBs^{-1}
6MHz
12MHz

802.4 Baseband — COAXIAL CABLE
DATA RATES
1 MBs^{-1}
5 MBs^{-1}
10 MBs^{-1}

802.5 Baseband — SHIELDED TWISTED PAIR
DATA RATE
1.4 MBs^{-1}

802.5 Baseband — COAXIAL CABLE
DATA RATES
4 MBS^{-1}
20 MBS^{-1}
40 MBS^{-1}

satisfy all the requirements, a number of LAN definitions were proposed, as listed below:

1. Bus LAN with CSMA/CD access, working at 10 Mb/s.

2. Bus LAN with token passing access.

3. Ring LAN with token passing access.

The committee also made various recommendations about transmission media covering most of the available types.

The aim of the proposals was to legitimise most of the popular LAN types and thus give users what they want without encouraging endless minor variations. It is interesting to note that in this respect, the proposed IEEE standards have therefore mostly defined something that already exists. For example, recommendation 1. above, for the CSMA/CD bus LAN, is very similar to the definition for Ethernet. In fact, since the proposals were published in 1982, this recommendation and the Ethernet definitions have both been altered so that they are now, to all purposes, identical.

Similarly, the recently published IBM proposals for a token-passing ring have much in common with recommendation 3. The close cooperation between the computer and telecommunications industries and the IEEE standards committee means that most of the major LAN manufacturers are going, at some stage, to conform with the IEEE standard.

However, there are at present no IEEE proposals covering anything resembling the Cambridge Ring LAN, which has caused some consternation in the UK, where the LAN originated. The Cambridge Ring and its derivatives have become popular, particularly in academic and scientific environments in the UK, and the possibility that it may now be adopted as one of the ISO's standards for LAN technology should ensure its survival.

Other standards bodies

As well as the ISO and the IEEE, a number of other organisations are looking at standards for LANs, in particular the European Computer Manufacturers Association (ECMA). In general the ISO and IEEE can be regarded as pacemakers in this particular field and any other organisations' standards are unlikely to vary greatly from theirs.

Defacto standards

For various reasons, some LANs are regarded as established (or de-facto) standards before any official recognition has been awarded to them. This is generally because they have been developed early on and adopted by a large number of users and manufacturers or because the manufacturer has such an important position in the field that their product cannot be ignored. The three LANs of interest here are Ethernet, the Cambridge Ring, and the proposed IBM token-passing ring.

Ethernet

Ethernet is discussed in detail elsewhere in the book so it will suffice to say here that because of its early development, by the Xerox Corporation, and its subsequent adoption by a consortium of important companies in the computing and telecommunications fields, it is one of the dominant LANs available. A number of suppliers sell their own version of it, and a greater number of manufacturers produce add-on components of various sorts, making it one of the few LANs which can be acquired in a modular form, from competing suppliers.

Its specification, however, ensures that Ethernet will not become one of the cheapest LANs available, no matter how many units are sold. It is a high-speed, versatile system and so hardware and software requirements are substantial.

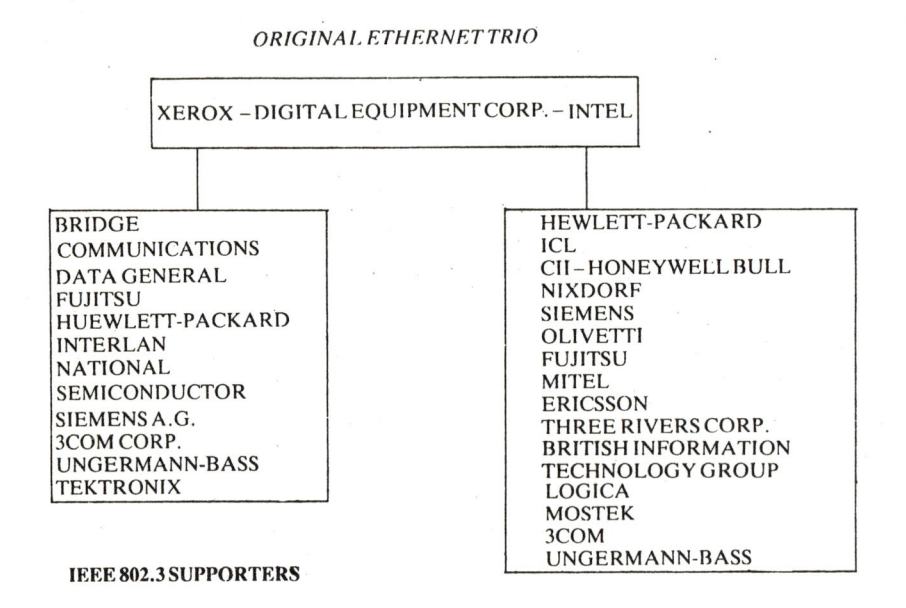

ORIGINAL ETHERNET TRIO

XEROX – DIGITAL EQUIPMENT CORP. – INTEL

BRIDGE	HEWLETT-PACKARD
COMMUNICATIONS	ICL
DATA GENERAL	CII – HONEYWELL BULL
FUJITSU	NIXDORF
HUEWLETT-PACKARD	SIEMENS
INTERLAN	OLIVETTI
NATIONAL	FUJITSU
SEMICONDUCTOR	MITEL
SIEMENS A.G.	ERICSSON
3COM CORP.	THREE RIVERS CORP.
UNGERMANN-BASS	BRITISH INFORMATION
TEKTRONIX	TECHNOLOGY GROUP
	LOGICA
	MOSTEK
	3COM
	UNGERMANN-BASS

IEEE 802.3 SUPPORTERS

ECMA STANDARD SUPPORTERS

Fig. 3.3 Ethernet consortium and associated organisations

The Cambridge Ring

Like Ethernet, the Cambridge Ring is examined in detail elsewhere in the book and we will just list the reasons for its predominance here. They are chiefly that it was developed early on as a scientific research network in the UK and most subsequent research involving LANs in academic and scientific circles has adopted the Cambridge Ring as its basic LAN because the expertise and software was freely available within this community. It has not had the same impact in the USA and so is unlikely to get recognition as an official standard there, but its recent acceptance by the ISO may lead to a revival of its fortunes. Meanwhile, a number of UK manufacturers have used it as the basis for the commercial LANs and it is enjoying some popularity.

IBM token-passing ring

IBM, the biggest computer manufacturer in the world, has after much deliberation recently announced its token-passing ring LAN as a product. The company proposed this type of LAN a considerable time ago but development has been slow. Because of the huge user base of IBM systems, and the size of the company, many observers expect the IBM LAN to become a de-facto standard when it is available, in the same way that the IBM Personal Computer quickly became the dominant PC, despite its relatively late introduction.

There is certainly a great deal of evidence to support this view but the fact remains that at the moment, the product is still not available. It is interesting to note that IBM are currently supplying a CSMA/CD broadband LAN for their PCs, which they have bought from another company (Sytek-q.v.) to fill what they obviously feel is a gap in their product range.

The IBM token-passing LAN is therefore a possible de-facto standard and, given the company's past history, must be looked at carefully by anyone working with IBM or IBM-compatible equipment.

Future trends

Observing the various official and de-facto standards mentioned above, it seems as if even the definers of standards cannot be prevailed upon to standardise amongst themselves.

However, there is no doubt that adoption by some sort of standards organisation gives any product a boost in the marketplace, and manufacturers will make strenuous efforts to see that their product is the one adopted. The other side of the coin is the fact that no defined standard has any real value unless it is adhered to by a substantial part of the group it is designed for. If a defined standard is inappropriate it will simply be ignored.

Which standards will flourish? A difficult thing to predict in detail but it is likely that a number of standards will continue to be supported at the top end of the market, where high-performance LANs will be required to serve a number of different special interests, such as process control and office automation. The assortment of IEEE 802 definitions take this into account and can therefore be expected to provide a guide for any future developments.

At the low-cost end of the market, with which we are more concerned, it is unlikely that LAN products will feel the need to conform with any of the published standards as it will always be more cost effective to produce a LAN designed for a specific application (e.g. file serving for up to 32 Apple IIes) from scratch than it will be to adopt a standardised high-power LAN for the purpose.

We will go into the problems associated with standards in more detail in the section dealing with specifying and purchasing LANs (Chapter 4).

CHAPTER 4

User Requirements: specifying and purchasing a LAN

This book has so far dealt with the theoretical background of LANs: the various types of design, the various standards, how the concept has developed, and so on. We now start to look at the practical side of matters, and in this chapter particularly, we will examine what a user might require from a LAN and how to specify and purchase a suitable network once user requirements have been defined.

What do you want from a LAN?

LANs serve a wide variety of functions and it is important that the prospective user is clear about what he requires from a LAN. For example it may be used to provide any or all of the following functions and many others:

>File serving
>Print serving
>Process control and monitoring
>Electronic messaging
>Distributed processing facilities
>Remote links to mainframe processors
>Conferencing
>Video transmission
>Electronic office functions

LAN applications are limited solely by the imagination of the user.

Very few systems can do all of these, and some LANs because of their nature will only perform a few of the functions well so it is useful to examine the system requirements for each type of application. In general, the following rules hold:

1. File and print servers. These are installed to spread the cost of expensive peripherals for groups of micro and mini computers and so low

49

interconnection costs are very important, with speed of operation being less so, particularly in the case of print servers.

2. Process control and monitoring. The vital factor in this application is the speed of the system response. The delay between the initiation of a command and its execution, or between the monitoring of an event and its acknowledgment by the process controller, must be short and fixed, so that the controller can make allowances for it. Thus a network with guaranteed access and short transmission delays is essential. Interconnection costs and equipment costs are not the overriding factor when the plant to which the LAN connects costs a great deal – much more than the LAN itself.

3. Electronic messaging. This function will normally be as an addition to local functions provided by small business computers and so must be compatible with them. Network traffic will be light compared with other applications and so a low speed network without guaranteed immediate access is indicated, as a time delay of a few seconds is not important in this application.

4. Distributed processing. Common in scientific and engineering work, where terminals, workstations and various sizes of computer are connected together in order to share software and hardware facilities. As programs and large batches of data need to be transferred from device to device at regular intervals, high speed bulk data transfer is the network's primary aim. Interconnection costs are not of primary importance, as the value of the attached equipment is usually relatively high.

5. Remote mainframe links. If this is the main purpose of the network, and a number of terminals wish to gain access to a single mainframe, network usage by each individual terminal will be low, and mainframe response time is likely to be much greater than network access time. A low speed network with variable access time will suit the application.

6. Conferencing. This application implies transmission of voice signals, as well as data, and therefore requires a network where speech can be transmitted in an analogue form e.g. PABX-based network, or one where speech can be digitised and then transmitted, without interrupting data transmission e.g. broadband network.

7. Video transmission. If video signals are to be transmitted as well as data, and possibly voice signals, the network must have a very high bandwidth and the ability to separate the various types of signal, or the video signal will be of unacceptably poor quality. This requires some sort of broadband system.

8. Electronic office functions. This covers a wide variety of functions including some mentioned above and so needs a reasonably high performance network to fulfil its requirements.

In addition, system limitations will affect the choice of LAN for many applications. For example, the following questions must be kept in mind when examining a LAN:

1. Can it support the number of nodes required? Most LANs have an upper limit on the number of devices that can be simultaneously attached to the network.

2. Can it cover the physical area of the site? Most types of LAN have an upper limit on the lengths of connecting cables. Some can be extended with repeater units but this will be an added expense.

3. Can the LAN cope with the maximum amount of traffic envisaged for the system in an acceptable manner? This question is less straightforward to answer than the previous two but ignoring it may prove a more costly mistake to rectify.

4. Can it be connected easily to the equipment with which it is to be used? LAN suppliers normally offer a variety of plug-in interface units for popular computers and peripherals, which make interconnection much simpler than would otherwise be the case.

Specifying a LAN

So far, we have thought about the purpose of the LAN and the types of system that will fulfil a particular purpose, but in a very general, broad way. It is now important to specify, in detail, without reference to any available commercial system, the network that is required. This is necessary at this stage to ensure that the network eventually purchased will meet the requirements of its users.

The best way to start is to follow this set of rules:

1. Draw up a list of the physical and logical requirements of the system:

    Number of nodes
    Area covered
    Maximum rate of data transfer
    Types of devices to be connected to the network
    Number of each type of device.

It is also worth drawing a plan of the layout to give a clearer idea of possible difficulties.

2. Find out from the potential users what they intend to do with the network and sort their responses into two types – essential requirements and optional extras.

3. Have a clear idea of the funds available, and the possibility of further funds for upgrading the LAN system at a later date.

Following these rules should give you a clear specification to present to any supplier of LANs and this is the most important stage in finding a system to suit your specific requirements.

However, at this point it is wise to consider whether a true LAN is the answer to your problems, or whether one of the various types of devices performing related functions might be a more cost-effective solution. It is unnecessarily expensive to pursue a high-tech solution when there is a low-tech one available.

For example, if the requirement is simply for a number of terminals or similar devices to be connected together, so that one device is only connected to one other device at any one time, in the manner of a telephone system, then an Intelligent Terminal Switch might be the answer, particularly if the physical distances are small. Other types of interconnection systems are compared and contrasted with LANs in the section on related devices (Chapter 6).

A LAN is probably the right answer if one or more of the following points are valid:

1. A wide variety of connections which change with time are required.

2. Cabling costs look like being a substantial proportion of system costs. LANs use the transmission medium efficiently and do not require multiple cables.

3. A large percentage of nodes in the system require regular access to other nodes i.e. most of the nodes have something to say at regular intervals.

4. Both point-to-point and broadcast data transmissions are required within the network. LANs need no alteration to physical connections to provide both.

Matching LANs to users

In the introduction we split LAN users into the following groups:

    Scientific and engineering
    Office automation
    Industrial automation/process control
    Education
    Home/interest

We will now examine their requirements and see which types of LAN serve them best. It is important to note that no two applications are alike and that the network should serve the user, rather than dictate what the user can and cannot do. For example, a network used for scientific or engineering purposes may well need to provide some services associated with office automation work, such as printing from a control station.

The three tables 4.1, 4.2 and 4.3 give comparisons of features for LANs assessed by transmission medium (4.1), accessing method (4.2) and topology (4.3). By listing the features most important for a particular application, it is possible to go a long way toward picking the most suitable type of LAN. The following two examples illustrate the process.

Transmission Medium	Bandwidth	Ease of Connection	Distance	Suitability for different topologies	Ease of installation	Noise Immunity	Cost
Twisted Pair	Low	Good	Low	High	Average	Low	Low
Baseband Coaxial	Average	Good	Average	High	Good	Average/good	Average
Broadband Coaxial	High	Good	High	High	Good	High	Average/High
Optical Fibre	Very High	Poor	Very High	Poor	Average	Very High	High

Table 4.1 Comparison of transmission media

Access Method	Nature	Bandwidth	No. of Nodes	Distance	Delay	Cost per Node
CSMA/CD	Random	High	Average	Average	Unlimited	High
Token Passing	Deterministic	Average	High	High	Low	Average
Register Insertion	Deterministic	Average/Low	High	High	Average/Low	Low
Empty Slot	Deterministic	Average	High	High	Low	Average
Time-Division-Multiplexed	Deterministic	Low	High	Average	Low	Low

Table 4.2 Comparison of access methods

53

Topology	Cost	Complexity at Interface	Flexibility and Expandability after installation	Reliability
Bus	Low/Average	Average	Good	Good
Ring	Average	Low	Average	Good
Star	High	Low	Poor	Average

Table 4.3 Comparison of topologies

Example 1: A network based in a school or college classroom, connecting a number of personal computers to a master computer operated by the teacher in charge, and to a print-serving device and a file-serving device. The master computer would not be in continuous communications with the rest but would need to access any of them from time to time. All would use print and file servers. The desired characteristics would be:

Transmission medium bandwidth	– low/moderate
no. of nodes	– low/moderate
distance	– low
ease of installation	– low/moderate
noise immunity	– low/moderate
cost	– low: the most important factor.
Accessing method control	– distributed (all intelligent nodes)
bandwidth	– low/medium
no. of nodes	– low/medium (dependent on class size)
distance	– low
degree of contention	– low
degree of determinism	– high
degree of flexibility	– low
delay time	– low/moderate
Topology interface complexity	– low (to keep costs low)
flexibility	– low
expandability	– low
reliability	– moderate to high
cost	– low * most important item.

Comparing the requirements with the tables suggests a bus or tree system with some sort of deterministic accessing scheme using twisted-pair cables. However, the evaluations in the tables are relative and it may prove that because of the relatively short distances involved, the extra cost of a different type of transmission medium may be negligible in comparison with the system cost. Similarly, the time delays involved in using a non-deterministic access method may be acceptable when considered in comparison with the speed the users interact with the various computer/nodes in the network.

Example 2: A network for a modern business office, where the current requirements are mainly linking an assortment of workstations, word-processors, print and file-servers but provision must be made for possible future expansion, and where links to the company mainframe and a video network are envisaged. Bearing in mind the final functions the LAN may have to perform, the desired characteristics would be:

Transmission medium bandwidth	– high (to accomodate video)
no. of nodes	– high (future additional nodes)
distance	– moderate (except for mainframe connection)
ease of installation	– moderate
noise immunity	– moderate
cost	– low * not most important factor
Accessing method control	– distributed
bandwidth	– high
no. of nodes	– high
distance	– moderate
degree of contention	– moderate
degree of determinism	– low
degree of flexibility	– high
delay time	– low and fixed (because of video)
Topology interface complexity	– can be high
flexibility	– high
expandibility	– high
reliability	– high
cost	– low (in comparison with system)

The network fulfilling the most conditions in this case would be a broadband coaxial, random access, bus or tree system, such as the commercial Ethernet (see section on Ethernet) LANs now being sold for office automation by a number of suppliers. There is however one problem: video transmission would require low, fixed time delays in transmissions, to avoid unacceptable degradation of the reconstituted video signal at the receiving station. This factor suggests that a deterministic access method i.e. some form of token-passing system, should be adopted to ensure future video compatibility, despite the reduced performance of the LAN in other areas that this choice of accessing method would imply.

On the subject of cost, cheaper is always better, but must be considered in terms of the cost of the system the LAN is to serve. One LAN may cost twice as much as another for a limited increase in facilities, but where this extra cost is only a few percent of the total system cost, it may well be acceptable.

Having decided which types of LAN will suit the specification, it is important to balance the trade-off between costs and features of suitable networks. It is rare that a LAN will provide everything its prospective users want at a price they are willing to pay and so some order of priority should be given to the various features in the specification. Beyond this point it is unwise to be specific as each application has its own pitfalls. The only sure result is that the final system will have some unnecessary features and not have some necessary ones, so allow for a certain amount of flexibility in your specification.

Purchasing a LAN

Having discovered a number of networks which seem to fulfil most or all of the specifications, the problem of choosing one to buy arises. A number of practical points can affect this decision.

1. Complete package or components? In other words, do you buy a 'turnkey' system from one supplier or various bits and pieces from different people, and then try to make them work yourself? The first course should guarantee a working system without too many problems, but will undoubtedly cost a great deal more than the latter option. Self-installation, in comparison, could be fraught with practical difficulties, which are covered in the practical installation section later in the book. In brief, do-it-yourself is only recommended if every penny counts, *and* there is adequate technical backup to solve the problems.

2. General compatibility. Really part of point 1., but worth looking at separately. A number of manufacturers supply LANs complete with workstations of their own design but do not provide interfaces for other popular makes of computer (e.g. IBM PC) or standard peripheral connections (e.g. Centronics interface, RS232C port, etc.) Purchasing this type of LAN is a quick way to get a network up and running but may make your current equipment redundant, or tie up expensive workstations as interface units to the equipment you wish to keep. In general, these packaged LAN-and-workstation systems are a good thing if an installation is being built from scratch, rather than networking existing devices. Most such LAN packages offer a standard operating system, such as CP/M, on their workstations and so a certain amount of software compatibility is catered for.

3. Timescale for delivery and installation. This can vary wildly from supplier to supplier and a more expensive or less versatile LAN may be a better buy if it can be installed now, when the delivery time for your first-choice LAN is six months or a year.

4. Where more than one LAN seems to fit the specification. Try to get the competing systems installed for a short time for evaluation purposes. Most suppliers will consider this if they feel it will lead to a sale. Despite matching your specifications to the suppliers', there is no substitute for the 'suck it and see' approach in assessing the usefulness of any piece of equipment.

5. Component costs may affect a decision. For example, if two LANs, one with coaxial cable and the other with fibre optic cable, suit your application and cost approximately the same amount, the component costs for future expansion are likely to be much greater for a fibre optic system than for a coaxial system. In this case, the coaxial cable system would be a better solution.

CHAPTER 5

Practical Installation

Theory and practice

Despite the best intentions and efforts of everyone involved, the installation and use of any high technology item of equipment rarely goes as planned. The variation between theory and practice can be a small nuisance or a huge, expensive disaster.

In this section, we will look at some of the more common difficulties encountered when installing a LAN and try to indicate how these can be avoided. Many of the problems described are common to all sorts of high-technology equipment and may well be worth remembering in other circumstances.

The gap between theory and practice occurs when the assessment of technical suitability fails to take into account the problems involved in installing the particular hardware (and possibly software in a modular system) which is required by the LAN, or when the operating conditions of the LAN deviate from the original specifications.

Common problems

The following problems break up into two main groups, as previously mentioned. The most common group is that produced by an inadequate original specification for the system. It is important to remember that items such as cabling are an integral part of the system and should be investigated and specified properly before a network is purchased. These are the main problem areas relating to poor specifications:

1. Cabling. In the area of cabling, the physical constraints imposed by the premises become immediately apparent. The network cables, either twisted pair, or coaxial, or fibre optic, must be routed to conform with current provisions for cables and in the case of the electrical conductors, be well clear of any electrical noise sources. This may well mean that it is difficult or impossible to have the cables emerging where they are required. Some of the coaxial cables e.g. Ethernet, are very stiff as they have a solid outer conductor, and are therefore restricted in the amount they can be bent. This may cause difficulties in installing them in standard cable ducts.

Positioning for the cable tap points, where the network nodes are attached to the cable, must be considered carefully to avoid problems.They should be placed as close to the networked equipment as possible, without interfering with associated equipment. However, it may be that spacing between the cable tap points must be maintained, depending on the type of network, and so more than one node may have to share the same cable tap point. Where a number of networked devices stand in the same area, they may overload the physical connection facilities of the network at that point.

At the other end of the scale, some nodes may be too far from the main network to be connected without exceeding the allowed distance for cabling. In some networks, this problem can be overcome by adding an extra length of cable and a repeater to boost and reconstitute the network signals but in others, it may be necessary to have the remote node as a separate system with a special connection to the main system. In either case, connection will be expensive, but there are ways round these problems if they can be indentified at the planning stage.

The distance limits set by manufacturers and suppliers for the full extent of their standard networks (typically 1/2 – 1 km.) may seem much greater than the user's needs, but the practical difficulties involved in installing a network will very quickly use up the available cable. By planning the optimum layout for the cable, the user can include a much greater area within the network. See Figs. 5.1, 5.2 for an example of optimising the cable layout for a bus LAN within a single multi-storey building.

Finally, on the subject of cabling, there is the matter of the robustness of the cable. In some situations, the cable may be exposed to damp and extreme temperatures, particularly where the network connects separate buildings. More commonly, it may be prone to mechanical damage where it is not protected by suitable cable ducting. The only answer in both these cases is to determine the possible dangers, minimise them as much as possible, and protect the cable or ensure that it can withstand any remaining dangers. It is difficult to be more specific but awareness of the dangers is the most important step towards averting them.

2. Operating Software. Software to operate the network, or rather the lack of it, is becoming less and less of a problem as more manufacturers offer a complete 'turnkey' system, which includes all the necessary hardware and software. With this type of LAN, it is only necessary to ensure that the software, like the hardware, will do all that is required of it. This can

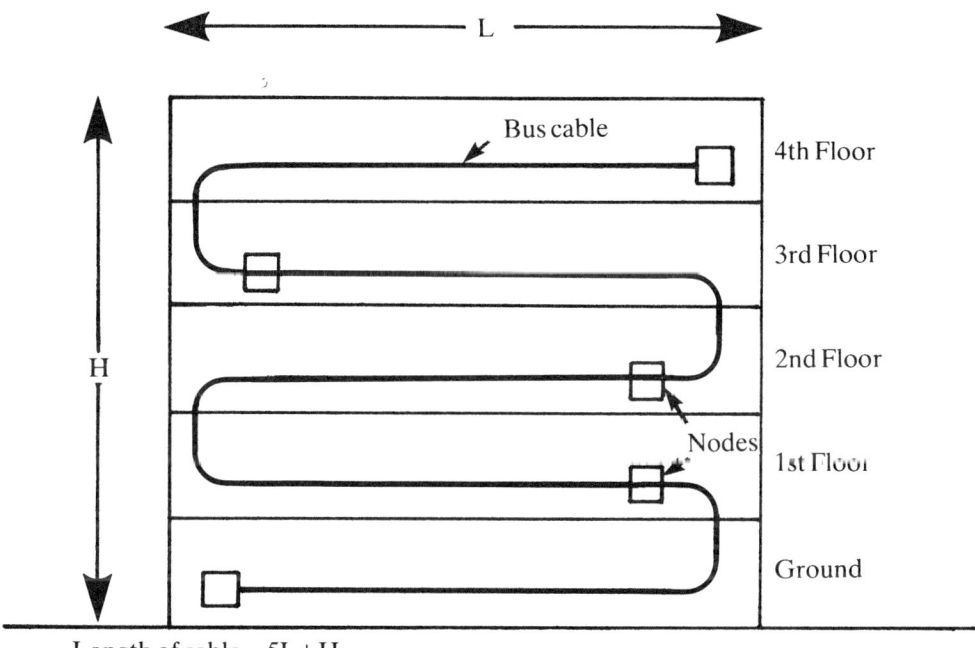

Length of cable = 5L+H

Fig. 5.1 Cable layout for five-storey building

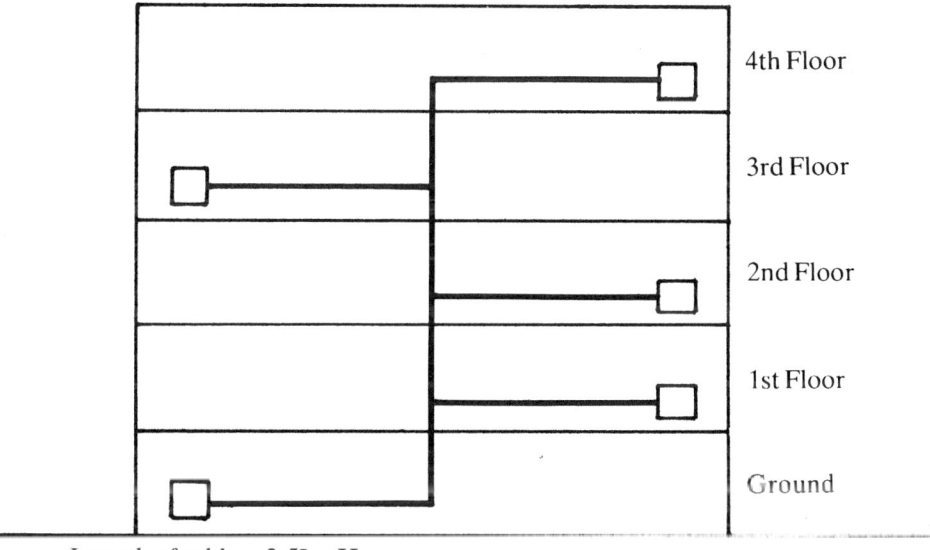

Length of cable = 2.5L+H

Fig. 5.2 Alternative cable layout to Fig. 5.1

normally be determined at an early stage by discussing the specification with the supplier. After this, any inadequacies in the software will be due to inadequate specifications, or must be rectified by the supplier.

LANs constructed from component parts produce a different set of problems, and are particularly prone to software difficulties. Software from two different suppliers is notoriously difficult to persuade to communicate with each other and this single problem of incompatible software may be the greatest hurdle in getting a LAN into operation. Again the only way to avoid this is to specify the operating parameters of each software package exactly and, where possible, test the software in advance under realistic conditions. There is no substitute for seeing a version of the network you are interested in working under similar circumstances to your own projected requirements.

In general, it is best to avoid any systems where the software must be tailored to operate as required. Even if the user can do this job, the time and expense involved make it an unattractive proposition unless there is no other possible solution.

3. Expandability. Again, the lack of this facility may create problems once the system is installed, particularly if the network performs well. It is always desirable to increase the usage of a LAN if it is seen to be successful and provision should be made at the planning stage for any possible extra uses of the system after it is commissioned. Expansion difficulties may be caused by any or all of the following:

(i) Lack of physical access points i.e. the number of cable tap points and positioning of the cable may be inadequate to allow extra devices to be connected to the network.

(ii) Lack of logical access points i.e. the system operating software may not provide sufficient logical nodes or unique addresses for all the devices requiring access to the LAN. This is a serious potential hazard if the software cannot be altered to suit an expanded network and prospective users should ensure that a network can provide access for all their future needs. Manufacturers' specifications for the maximum number of nodes allowed vary tremendously but usually increase in proportion to system cost.

(iii) Lack of data-carrying capacity i.e. the network may be able to support extra devices but adding them to the LAN degrades its performance to an unacceptable level. This will happen in any LAN as the actual combined data transmission rates of the attached nodes approaches the quoted data transmission rate of the network. As this point is reached, more data is being generated by the nodes than the network can transmit, and so the data must join a queue until the network is ready for it. This phenomenon is familiar to users of large mainframe computers when the computer is overloaded and can result in serious delays which make the system difficult to use.

All three of the points mentioned here must be noted if the network is to be expanded successfully in the future. Additionally it should be possible to add extra cabling to the system without unnecessary expense or difficulty. This will allow both for expansion and for alternative uses of the network, when equipment is moved and used in new locations.

4. Standardisation. Where the LAN is supplied complete with workstations, standardisation of interfaces will not be a problem. If, however, you are looking at a LAN to interconnect existing equipment, it is vital that the LAN nodes can be connected to the equipment without difficulty. This implies some sort of standard interface unit compatible with the interface units on the existing equipment.

There are a number of standard, or rather generally accepted, forms of connection available on the types of equipment likely to be used as workstations, file-servers or print-servers in the network. The most common will be some form of serial data link using RS232C/V24 protocols, simple 8-bit parallel data links like the Centronics interface standard, or more complex 8-bit parallel data links like the IEE488 interface bus. The last is very common in programmable test and measurement equipment.

If the LAN under examination is to be used for a variety of equipment and does not provide interfaces for some or all of the standards mentioned above, it is unlikely to be suitable.

A number of commercially-available LANs are designed for use with specific microcomputers, such as the Apple IIe, or IBM PC, and include interface units that plug directly into the expansion sockets in the microcomputer. These networks normally allow other devices to be attached via interfaces in the microcomputer and are thus versatile in terms of the range of compatible equipment. However, each extra device attached to the network requires a microcomputer to act as an interface unit and so it is an expensive proposition to add new items as an extra microcomputer will be tied up servicing the new item. See Fig. 5.3.

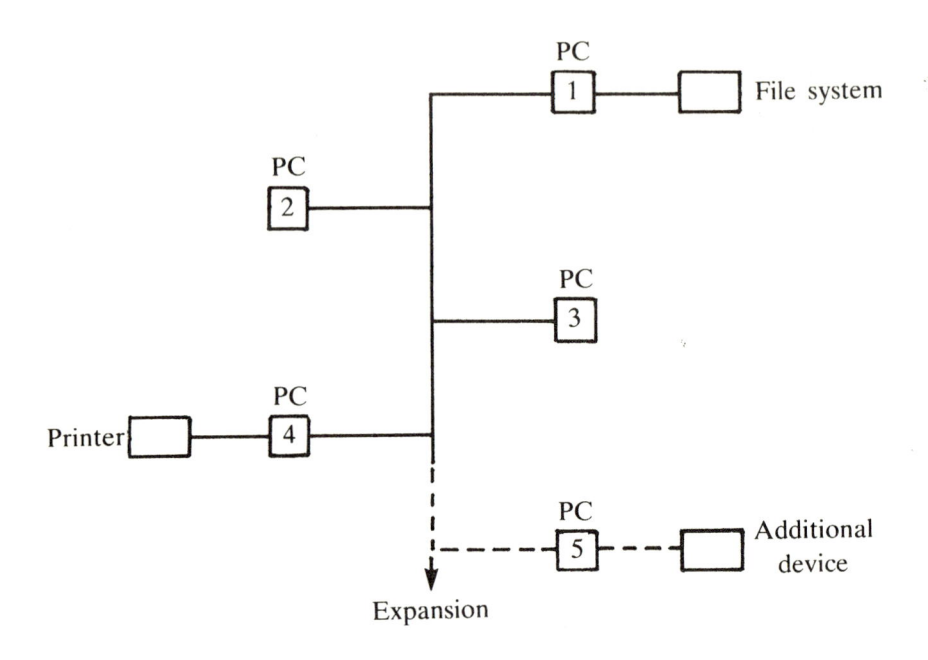

Fig. 5.3 Problems inherent in LANs dedicated to single types of microcomputers

In general, standardisation of interconnections can be a serious problem for modular LANs used to interconnect existing equipment, but is unlikely to be a significant installation and operation problem in turnkey systems.

As use of the network changes, other difficulties may arise. Matters such as expandability and overloading have already been touched upon as consequences of poor specifications but they will become acute if the way the network is used changes with time, particularly as more potential users see the advantages of applying the installed LAN to their requirements. It is therefore vital that manufacturers and suppliers provide technical support both during installation and operation of the LAN. A good supplier should be happy to have a representative on site throughout the installation period and continue to make engineers available if there are any problems after installation is complete.

CHAPTER 6

Related systems

There are a number of systems which appear, at first examination, as LANs or something similar, but do not qualify under the definitions we used earlier. The most interesting and relevant of these are the following:

>Private telephone exchanges (PABXs)
>Intelligent terminal switches (ITS)
>Wide area networks (WANs)

These terms in themselves cover a variety of systems and we shall examine them in the light of their relationship to LANs, and how they can be used to supplement or replace a LAN.

There are other kinds of networking systems which are normally designed and used for a specific purpose – for example, high-speed data links between pairs of mainframe computers, but these mostly lack the elements of versatility and cheapness that we are particularly interested in, and do not have a general applicability of design which would make them interesting from a technical point of view, unlike the three main categories of systems related to LANs at which we will look.

PABX

The Private Automatic Branch Exchange, or PABX as it is normally termed, has been seen by many people as the best medium for LAN-type operations in most modern circumstances. PABXs are installed in most office and factories of any size and are in constant use connecting telephone users to other users both on the site and outside it. A user can connect to any other user simply by dialling the required number, which is analagous to a LAN node transmitting data to another node and identifying the destination of the data by means of an address.

A PABX can be characterised as a circuit-switched star network transmitting analogue data at audio frequencies. A typical layout is shown in Fig. 6.1. To operate the system, the user dials the number of the telephone he wishes to reach and this dialling information is used by the PABX to set up the correct routing for the call. If the call is successful, the circuit is held

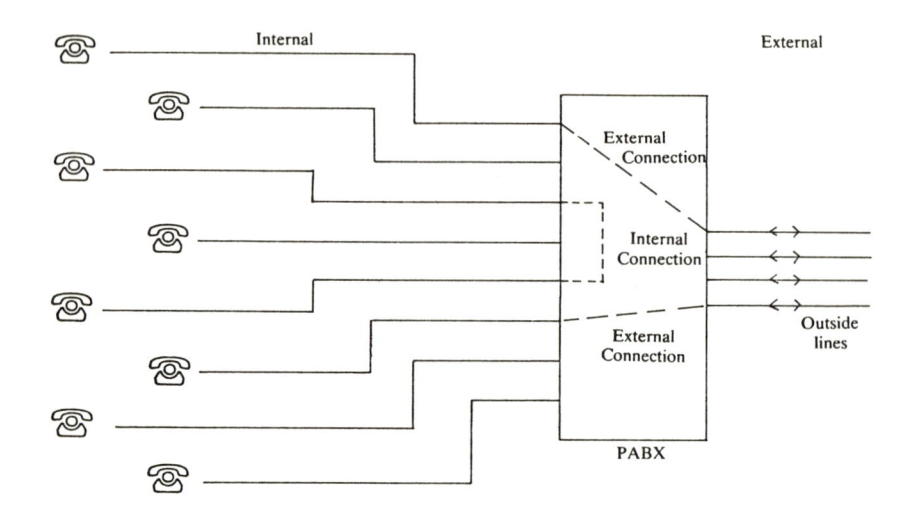

Fig. 6.1 Typical PABX layout

until both ends replace the receiver, at which time the central PABX breaks the circuit. This means a PABX-type system is very efficient at setting up one-to-one communications. However, it may be difficult to organise broadcast (one-to- many) data transmissions as the internal switching circuits may not allow multiple connections. A normal star network will have a central controller to which all nodes can talk simultaneously but again, this will not be the case in a PABX network as the central device exists purely to switch connections, and does no data processing.

Modern PABXs have replaced the original electromechanical switches used in old exchanges with software-controlled, solid state devices and are in fact now computers which are configured for channel switching. This means that, in theory at least, PABXs can operate in a packet-switching mode, as well as a circuit-switching mode. The necessary modifications will only be in the software, provided that the system is well-designed.

The voice information carried by the cables of a normal PABX is low-frequency (typically 300-3000 Hz) and so the cables are twisted-pair types, which are cheap and limited to slow data rates in comparison with the coaxial types used in most LANs. To send digital data along these lines, it is common to use a modem (MOdulator and DEModulator) which employs the digital data to modulate a carrier signal designed to suit the signal-carrying characteristics of the cable. The digital data is extracted from the carrier at the receiving end by a reverse process of demodulation. Because normal voice transmission contains an echo, it is necessary to arrange data transmission in a PABX-based LAN so that this echo, which is more accurately termed a transmitted signal fed back to the transmitter, is ignored or supressed. This is important if echoed data is not to be confused with fresh data transmitted from the far end of the link. Echo suppression, which recognises the echoed signal and cancels it out, or burst mode transmission, where the two users talk alternately at a fixed rate, both allow the telephone link to be used satisfactorily as a 2-way data link, although they require more circuitry than a standard modem arrangement.

It would seem that the prospects for turning a PABX into a true LAN are not good, if all the modifications and difficulties listed above are taken into account. To counter all these reasons for not trying to convert a system designed for one purpose into a multipurpose network, PABX supporters argue that the most important asset of a PABX is its installed wiring. Installing wiring for a LAN may well be the major cost of the network, and the fact that a PABX-based LAN will have its wiring already installed can outweigh the difficulties involved in converting the central exchange to a digital PABX.

One serious drawback of any star network is the vulnerability of the central section of the system – the hub – to breakdown. If the hub fails, the system fails completely, unlike an equivalent bus or ring network, where node failure allows other nodes to operate unhindered. To avoid the potential disasters that could occur with hub failure, the central device must be extremely reliable. This is certainly the case with PABXs which have to pass the most stringent test of reliability.

PABXs can grow to look like LANs in a number of distinct stages, which range from a standard PABX containing a small number of switched digital data lines, to a fully digitised, packet-switched voice and data LAN. A basic PABX can accommodate digital data lines without too much difficulty, requiring only a set of modems and some means of dialling the required connection. This can be a normal handset which is then used in conjunction with an acoustic coupler modem to transmit data (Fig. 6.2). The circuit is released by replacing the handset. In this set-up, the PABX itself is unchanged and data transmission is made possible by the addition of external devices.

The next stage in sophistication would be the use of data terminals incorporating hard-wired, rather than acoustically-coupled modems to replace ordinary telephone handsets where digital data transmission only was required. These data terminals would also contain auto-dialling circuits which would set up the PABX connection on command from the attached

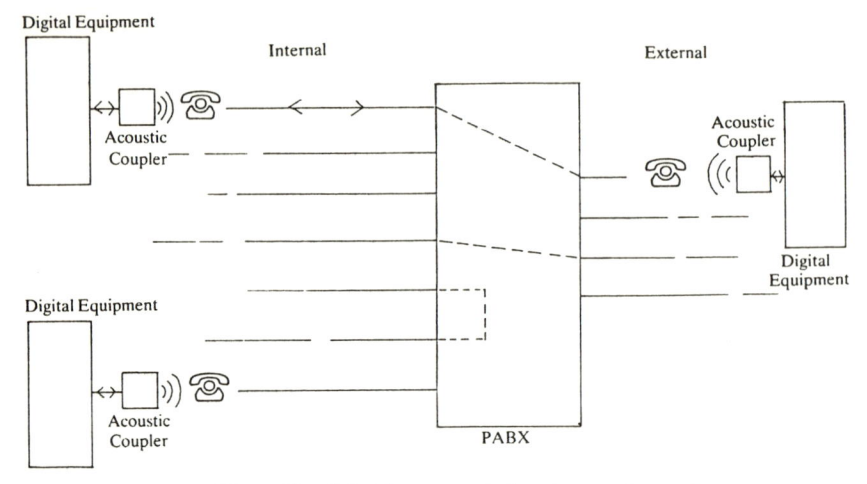

Fig. 6.2 PABX used for digital data transmission via acoustic couplers

device e.g computer, visual display unit. In this system, the central exchange unit would remain unchanged and still operate in circuit-switched mode. Circuit release would be accomplished by the data terminal. (Fig. 6.3.)

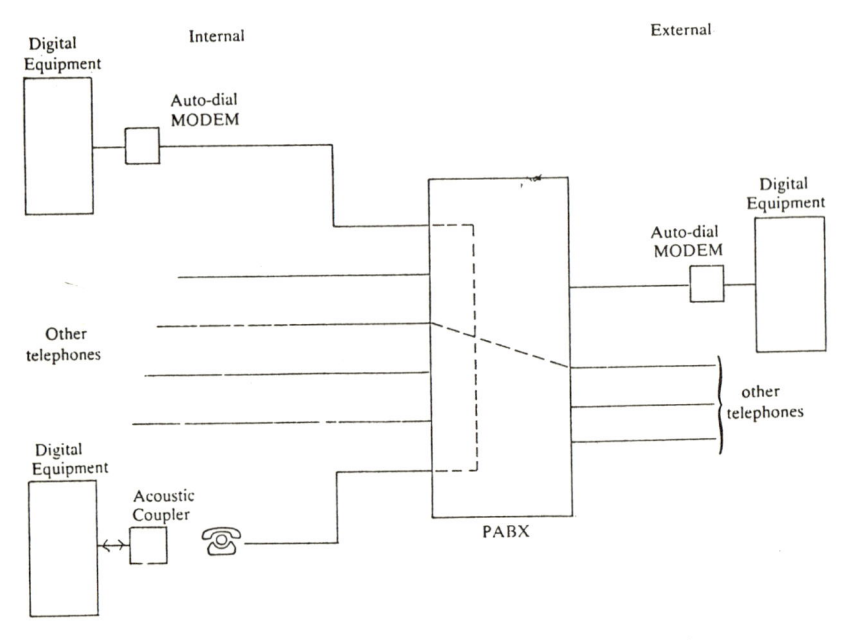

Fig. 6.3 PABX used for digital data transmission via hard-wired modems

A fully-digital voice and data PABX-based LAN would again use data terminals as access points to the network but would have the central exchange reconfigured to work in packet-switching mode. In addition voice data would be digitised as it entered the network and then transmitted to its destination as a series of packets of digital data. It would be reconstituted into its original form at the receiving data terminal and passed on to the receiving handset. This fully-digital packet-switched LAN would have the advantage of being able to treat all data in the same manner, and also be able to broadcast data packets (one-to-many) and allow one user to receive data from a number of sources simultaneously (many-to-one transmission). In fact, the simultaneous transmissions would be achieved by switching packets of data very quickly but this will appear as simultaneous transmission to the user, if the packets are small. (Figure 6.4.)

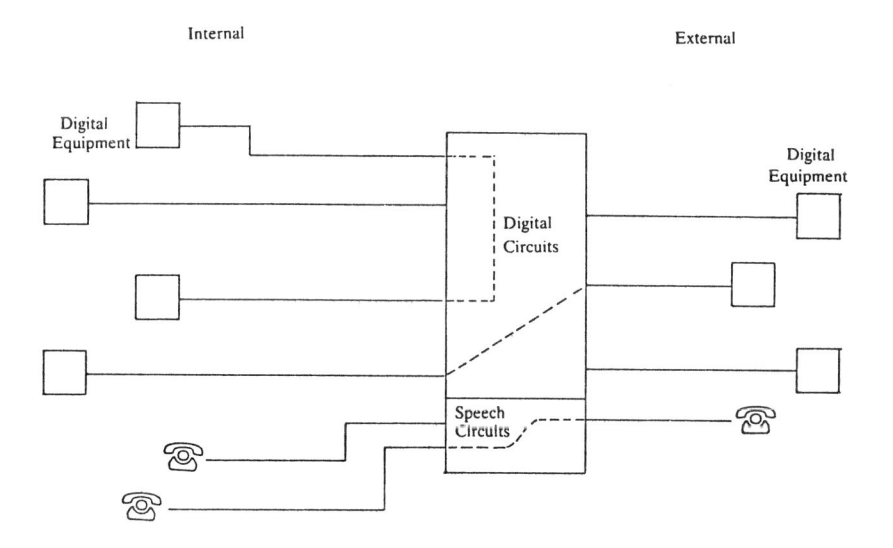

Fig. 6.4 PABX as combined speech and data network

The advantages and disadvantages of using a PABX as the basis for a LAN are listed below:

Advantages:

>Wiring already installed in normal circumstances.
>Combined voice and data transmission.
>Immediate access once connection is made.
>Large areas and high aggregate speeds are possible.

Disadvantages:

Central exchange failure halts the whole network.
Central exchange is complex and costly.
Channel-switched PABXs may cause long delays if the selected destination is already engaged.
Relatively low-speed transmission in each branch of the network.

Interestingly, the PABX-based LAN allows high aggregate data rates whilst restricting individual channel speeds, which is the reason for the seemingly – contradictory entries in advantage and disadvantage tables. This is possible because of the large number of separate connections in the central exchange. If these are used to allow device A to talk to device B, and so on, the aggregate speed of data is the sum of the speeds of connections AB, CD, etc. In this sort of multiple one-to-one communication, a PABX is an effective method of making connections.

It seems, therefore, that in certain circumstances a PABX can perform as a LAN and a great deal of research is currently being undertaken to produce PABXs which are suitable for LAN functions, thus doing away with two coexisting and overlapping systems. This type of LAN will have distinct advantages in the fields of voice transmission and man-computer interaction i.e. transmission of data to and from VDUs and Teletypes, but will be less useful for high-speed transfer of large amounts of data without expensive additions to the basic network. It may, therefore, emerge in the future as one of the main types of LAN used in office environments.

Intelligent terminal switches

The term 'intelligent terminal switch' is used to cover a variety of devices used variously as communications servers, data concentrators, or multiplexes.

All these configurations are based on what are essentially PABX-type devices which have been conceived from the beginning as purely digital, medium-to-high speed, packet-switched devices. They are normally designed to act as interfaces to larger systems (Figure 6.5) or to concentrate data from a number of devices onto a single line for high-speed transmission (Figure 6.6).

Many of these devices, particularly the more modern and sophisticated of them, are also able to switch data transmission from terminal to terminal, thus providing some of the functions of a star network LAN.

Where user requirements for a network are not strenuous, an ITS may be a more cost-effective solution as they are generally much cheaper than a true

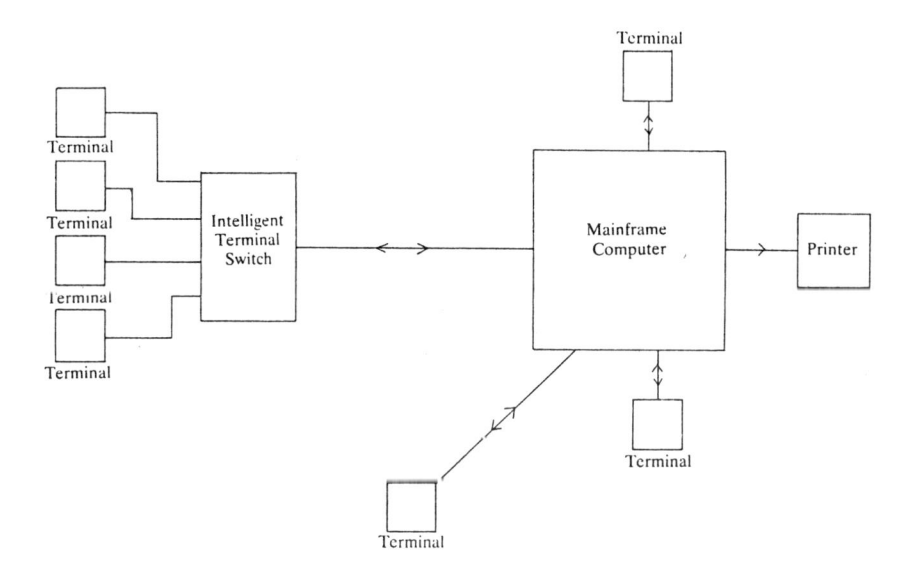

Fig. 6.5 Intelligent terminal switch as access point to larger system

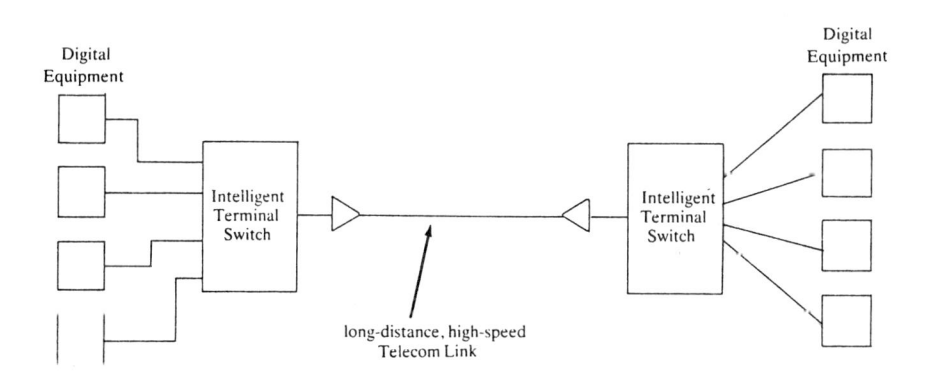

Fig. 6.6 Intelligent terminal switch as data concentrator

LAN covering the same area. However, they are unlikely to provide the same level of services, and in an environment where broadcast data, mailbox services, error detection and correction, etc, are required, it is unlikely that an ITS will fulfil the requirements.

The limited and fixed services of a typical ITS network should be compared with the user's requirements in order to determine its suitability for a particular application.

One area where intelligent terminal switches will develop is as servers or gateways to high-powered networks, where they can be used to concentrate a number of simple devices into one LAN node, thus spreading the network node cost over a number of devices, as well as allowing a certain amount of direct communication between attached devices. This is particularly attractive in LANs such as Ethernet, where the cost of a node may well be more than that of the attached device if it is a printer or terminal. This system of interconnections can also be used to construct gateways from one kind of network e.g. between a LAN and WAN, or between a LAN and a PABX.

It is likely, therefore, that intelligent terminal switches will appear within and alongside true LANs, as well as existing on their own, for some time to come.

Wide area telephone networks

In the early days of computing, the computers themselves were large, expensive and immovable. So much so that if someone wanted to use a computer in their work there was little or no possibility of them having one of their own. The potential user had to either travel to the computer to work with it or install a data link between his workplace and the computer. The cost of remote data links, even over public telephone networks, were much smaller than the cost of the computer, and it seemed a satisfactory solution.

Gradually, the technology was developed to allow a large number of terminals to talk to the mainframe computer thus creating long-distance, or wide-area, networks. Since the advent of relatively cheap personal computing (including minicomputers), the need for this type of WAN is not as apparent, but wide area networks are also used to connect large computers together and in certain circumstances can be used to interconnect separate LANs, allowing LAN users access to external resources.

The usual transmission medium for a WAN is the public telephone network However, some recent systems transmit data via satellite links. One example of this new approach is Project Universe, which has been set up to interconnect the LANs of a number of British universities and research establishments. The centres use standard LAN technology on site by means of a geostationary satellite link (Figure 6.7). The satellite connection is backed up with an X25 gateway to normal telecoms links.

Two new developments have encouraged WAN projects in recent years. One is the portable personal computer, which can be taken away from the

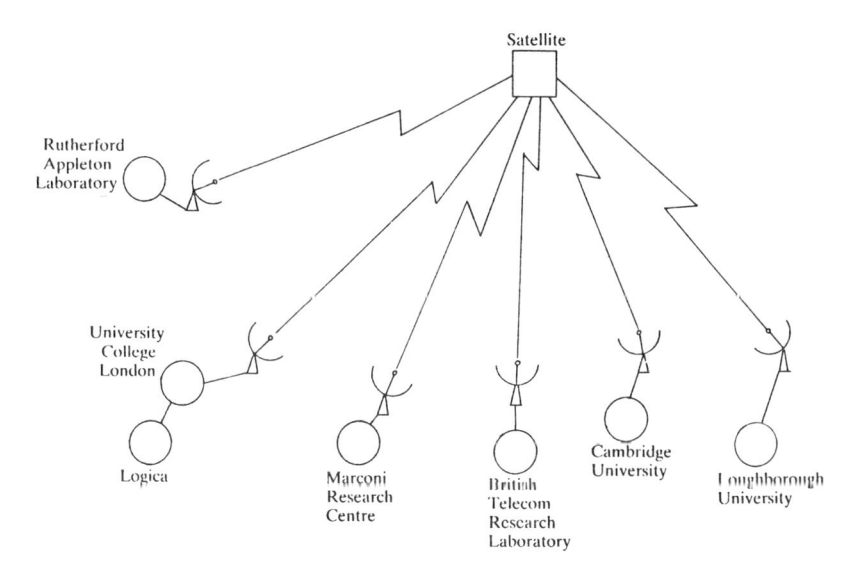

Fig. 6.7 Project UNIVERSE

office by a business user for work on site, on business trips, or at home. In order to keep in contact with the main office facilities at a distance, many users of portable business microcomputers resort to modems through which they can have access to the company computer over normal telephone lines, thus hopefully improving their effectiveness and productivity. The new generation of portable business microcomputers are being produced with integral modems, giving some indication of the increasing interest in this new field.

The other new development encouraging WAN operation, is the advent of 'Value-Added Networks' or VANs. These are centralised data services to which subscribers can gain access via telephone lines and use for their own purposes. A typical VAN would be a data base of specialised and constantly-updated information which a subscriber could interrogate for his own particular requirements, such as the service travel agents use to determine package holiday availability.

The most common UK VAN is Prestel, a database service containing a variety of information. Subsections, or 'pages', of the database are hired by various organisations and filled with information of interest to particular groups of subscribers, who pay a fee for access to individual pages, as well as for the complete Prestel service.

The database and mailbox services provided by Prestel, Telecom Gold and similar VAN system can be used to cover any conceivable subject or interest, and one of the recently-introduced Prestel services is aimed specifically at home microcomputer users. Most Prestel users have special-purpose microcomputer/modem combinations which are designed for, and will only function within, their own particular area of interest. Micronet 800, however, is designed for home computer users to extend the functions of their microcomputer, by providing a range of network functions which were previously the domain of large expensive computer systems. These include electronic mail, interchange of software, and bulletin boards.

The subscriber is provided with a modem by Micronet and is thus given cheap, quick access to the complete Micronet 800 system. As the supply of cheap modems increases, private network services are springing up internationally. Some are professional services designed to meet particular needs and make a profit. Many more are free bulletin board services run from a private telephone and available to anyone who wants to send or receive a message. These latter systems are surely an indication that the technology involved in networking over British Telecom's links has come of age and is now available to any prospective user.

A full treatment of wide-area networking for microcomputers and the possibilities it opens up is beyond the scope of this chapter, but it is clear that the independence it provides for small computer users will be an important factor in the future, leading to a number of uses not discussed here, and probably not yet imagined by the current users of the technology.

CHAPTER 7
Research Networks

Introduction

Much of the original development work concerned with local area networking was carried out before LANs were regarded as a commercial proposition. These early investigations were prompted by academic curiosity, or by a need to produce a data communication network to fulfil unusual requirements in research work, which could not be met by the available communications technology of the time.

This early work led on to a number of different types of network, with most possible combinations being considered at one time or another, but there are two main types of network which have grown from research beginnings into widely-accepted standards. These are the Ethernet type, and the Cambridge Ring type.

We shall be examining both in detail shortly, but for now, a quick specification will serve to identify these two very different types of network.

Ethernet:

Topology	– bus (branching non-rooted tree)
Medium	– coaxial cable
Access Method	– CSMA/CD
Speed	– 10MB
Range	– 2.5Km
No. of nodes	– 1024
Band	– baseband

Cambridge Ring:

Topology	– ring
Medium	– twisted pair
Access Method	– empty slot
Speed	– 10MB
Range	– >1km
No. of nodes	– 254
Band	– baseband

Ethernet

Ethernet, as it exists today, was first designed and installed by the Xerox Corporation at its Palo Atto Research Centre (PARC) in the mid-1970s, but its theoretical forebears go back to a network set up by the University of Hawaii called ALOHA. The University of Hawaii has campus sites scattered throughout the Hawaiian Islands and telephone links were considered too slow and unreliable for connecting computers and terminals between the various sites. The University's computer centre decided to use radio broadcast as the transmission medium for interconnection of their equipment, which resulted in a network where any station with data to transmit would broadcast it immediately, and only know if it was received correctly when the receiving station transmitted an acknowledgement.

This is a forerunner of CSMA/CD access methods, but the transmitting stations broadcast without observing the transmission medium, and can only therefore detect a collision, or other form of corruption of the transmitted packet of data, if an acknowledgement is not received within a certain time. To this end, an internal timer is set at the transmitting station every time a packet is transmitted, and the packet will be retransmitted when the time period expires.

ALOHA uses radio braodcast, rather than some form of cable, as its transmission medium, and covers a very large area – the distance between islands is much greater than a typical LAN site – but is otherwise essentially a LAN. The Xerox Corporation incorporated a lot of its features into the experimental LAN installed at PARC from which the current Ethernet standard was developed.

The initial installation was designed to connect office equipment and workstations to shared resources such as printers and large computers and worked so successfully that other Xerox sites and other organisations adopted Ethernet as a solution to their data communication problems and it came to be seen as a de-facto standard for LAN development. This culminated in 1980 in a joint specification for an uprated version of Ethernet being issued by Xerox in conjunction with the Digital Equipment Corporation and Intel. The support of three of the semiconductor/computer industry's heavyweight manufacturers encouraged a number of other prominent companies to support Ethernet as an industry standard, and band together into what is commonly referred to as the 'Ethernet Consortium' (see Fig. 3.3).

When the American Institute of Electrical and Electronic Engineers (IEEE) published its recommendations for LANs, referred to as IEEE 802 standards after the number of the LAN standards committee, one of them was almost identical with the Ethernet Consortium specification and it is expected that the Ethernet specifications will be quickly brought into line with the IEEE standards in all respects. This effectively means that Ethernet has the support of one of the most important standards organisations in the industry and thus seems set for a long and successful life.

A large number of manufacturers are now producing Ethernet components under licence, making it one of the few LANs which can be assembled in what is effectively a kit form. The possibility of buying similar components from different suppliers frees the user from the dangers of being 'locked-in' to one manufacturer, and as the economies of scale allow semiconductor manufacturers to integrate more Ethernet functions into a single component, prices should drop dramatically.

Ethernet specification

The information in this section is based on the Ethernet Data Link and Physical Layer Specification, Version 1.0 published in 1980 by the Xerox Corporation.

Ethernet is designed to do the following things:

1. To be simple – features which would complicate the design without improving performance are omitted.

2. To be low-cost – in order to be a suitable medium for interconnection of equipment whose cost continues to fall, Ethernet itself should be cheap.

3. To allow compatibility of all Ethernet installations – the specification avoids optional features, thus allowing any Ethernet station to communicate directly with any other, at physical link and data link levels. (See OSI specification, Chapter 3.)

4. To allow single nodes, groups, or the whole network to be addressed by a transmission.

5. To allow all nodes equal access to the network, on average.

6. To prevent any node interfering with the proper functioning of any other node.

7. To be high-speed – the network should operate at a data rate of 10MBits/second.

8. To be stable – the network performance in terms of data successfully transmitted should not degrade as the amount of data for transmission increases. In other words the system should not clog up as the load increases.

9. To keep delays to a minimum – no data should be kept waiting longer than necessary for transmission.

10. To have a layered architecture – the physical and data link layers specified are completely independent and correspond to the two lowest layers of the OSI model (Chapter 3).

Ethernet does not do the following things:

1. Provide full-duplex communication. Only one device can talk at once. The appearance of two-way communication can only be provided by two devices talking alternately in rapid succession.

2. Provide Error Control. The layers specified only detect bit errors and collisions. Recovery from these and other errors must be handled by the higher layers of the network.

3. Provide Security. There is no encryption or restricted access implied in this specification.

4. Provide variable speeds. The network operates at 10Mbits/second.

5. Provide a priority control. All nodes have equal access rights to the network.

The transmitted data must be in a specific format, referred to as a 'frame' (see Fig. 7.1) and must be in Manchester Code. As Fig. 7.1 shows, the frame contains a great deal more than the data which is its reason for existence. The other information transmitted consists of the following segments in order:

1. Destination Address. This comprises six bytes, referred to as 'octets' in the Ethernet literature, with the first bit set to 0 if the address is a 'physical' or unique address, and set to 1, if the frame is being 'multicast' i.e. being transmitted to a group of receivers. The remaining 47 bits form an address identifying the destination. All these bits are set to 1 if the message is being 'broadcast' i.e. sent to every receiver in the system.

2. Source Address. This field also comprises six bytes, with the first bit always set to 0, since the physical/multicast address distinction is irrelevant.

3. Type. Used by the higher levels of the OSI structure for identification purposes. Its contents depend on the protocols used by the controlling software. Consists of 2 bytes.

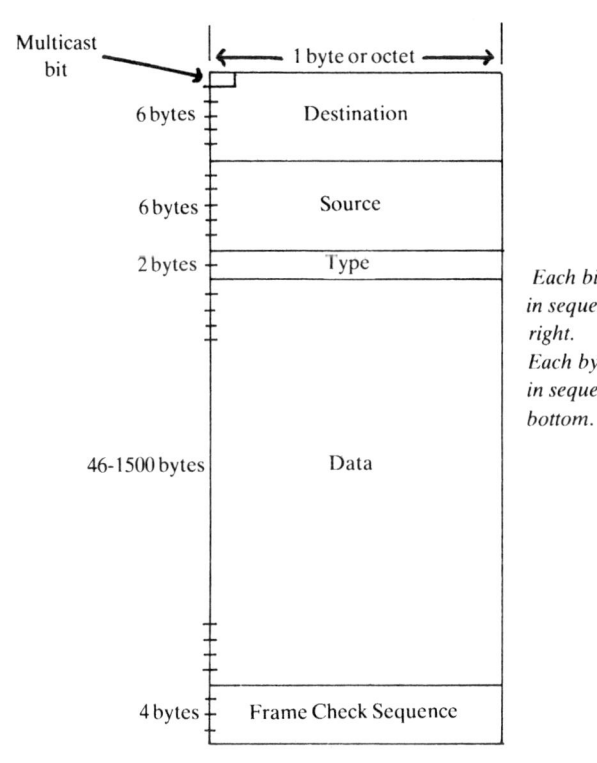

```
                    |←— 1 byte or octet —→|
    Multicast
      bit  ─────→ ┌─┬─────────────────────┐
              6 bytes │    Destination       │
                    ├─────────────────────┤
              6 bytes │      Source          │
                    ├─────────────────────┤
              2 bytes │       Type           │
                    ├─────────────────────┤        Each bit is transmitted
                    │                     │        in sequence from left to
                    │                     │        right.
                    │                     │        Each byte is transmitted
                    │                     │        in sequence from top to
                    │                     │        bottom.
          46-1500 bytes │       Data           │
                    │                     │
                    │                     │
                    │                     │
                    ├─────────────────────┤
              4 bytes │ Frame Check Sequence │
                    └─────────────────────┘
```

Fig 7.1 Ethernet frame format

4. Data. The information the frame has been created to transfer. It can be between 46 and 1500 bytes, and its contents are dependent entirely on the user.

5. Frame check sequence. This consists of four bytes which provide a cyclic redundancy check (CRC) of the preceding contents of the frame. The receiving software can use this to detect errors in transmission.

The frame proper is preceded by an 8-byte 'preamble' which is used to synchronise the receiving stations. It consists of the sequence '10' repeated 31 times followed by the sequence '11' transmitted once. The '10' sequence effectively generates a 5MHz square wave in the LAN, and the final two bits indicate that the frame proper is about to arrive. The frame follows immediately at the end of the preamble.

The address and type fields are controlled by the Xerox Corporation and are assigned to Ethernet patent licensees, or on request to other parties. This will ensure that all Ethernet addresses are unique and thus, in theory, Ethernet LANs may be interconnected and expanded without any problems of duplication or contention.

The topology of an Ethernet LAN can grow and alter through various stages from the simple system of Fig. 7.2 with only one cable segment, to the fully expanded system of Fig. 7.3 where a large number of cable segments are joined together.

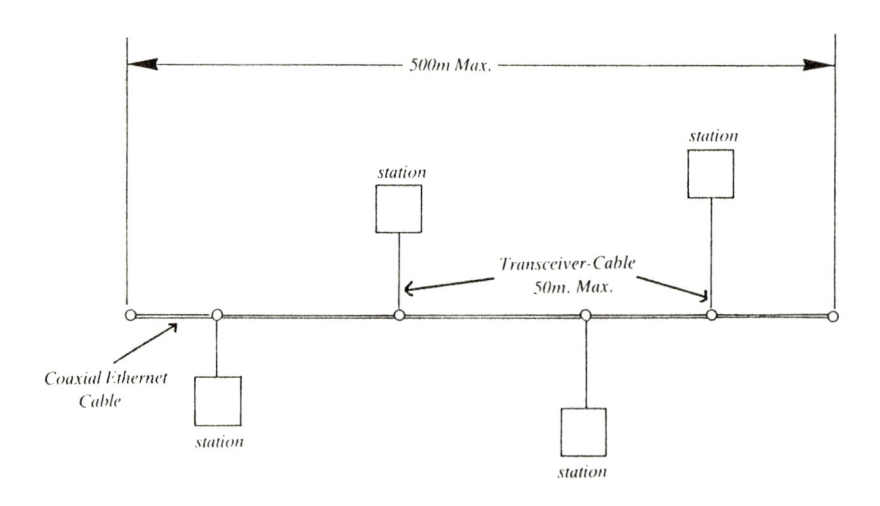

Fig. 7.2 Minimal Ethernet system

The factors constraining the physical layout of an Ethernet system are as follows:

1. Maximum coaxial cable segment length – 500m.

2. Maximum number of transceivers connected to a single cable segment – 100.

3. No more than two repeaters in the signal path between any two stations.

4. Maximum coaxial cable distance between two transceivers – 1500m.

5. Maximum length of transceiver cable between a transceiver and associated station (including repeaters) – 50m.

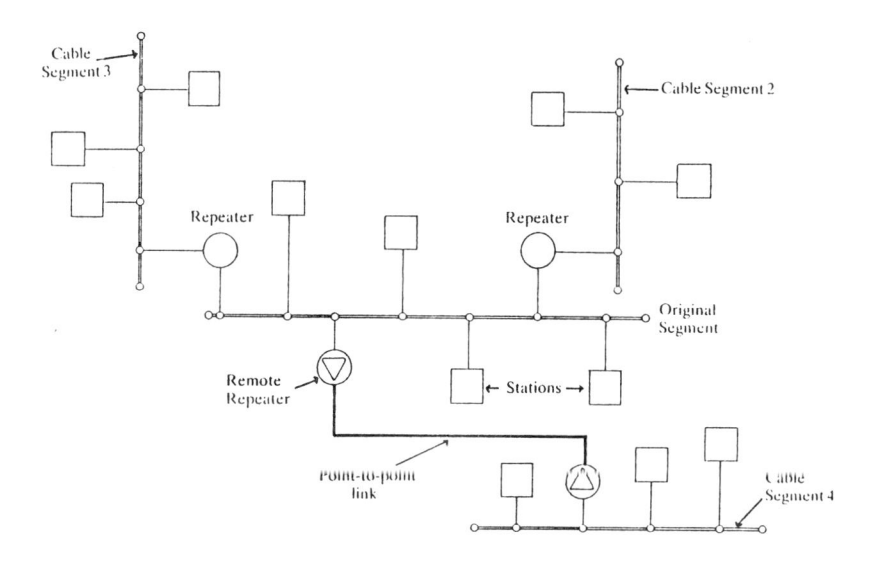

Fig. 7.3 Typical expanded Ethernet system

6. Maximum length of point-to-point link cable between any two stations in the system – 1000m.

The foregoing gives some idea of the physical operation of Ethernet. The uses to which it is put depend entirely on the user and the controlling software in the devices attracted to the network. A large number of manufacturers now produce Ethernet LANs or components, but there is no guarantee of compatibility unless the higher levels of the OSI model, of which Ethernet comprises the lowest two levels, are implemented in the same way at both ends of the link. In other words, Ethernet, despite its assurance of physical and data link compatibility, can still produce software compatibility problems when components from various sources are brought together.

Ethernet's great advantage is the support it has from a wide range of software and hardware manufacturers, such as the Digital Equipment Corporation, who will be working hard to provide a universally – compatible software environment in the future.

The Xerox Corporation originally envisaged Ethernet as a LAN primarily for office automation and the first installation at PARC was in an office environment. A great deal of the marketing effort since it became a commercial product has also been in the office automation field, for which it does indeed seem a viable system. However, the future trends in office automation seem to indicate a large increase in voice and video information traffic, on top of the present, purely digital, data transmission.

Xerox have experimented with speech transmission and had acceptable results, but the bandwidth of speech is much smaller than that of video by at least three orders of magnitude. It seems unlikely, therefore, that Ethernet will provide a real-time video transmission service, as the original specification did not concern itself with this area of data transmission.

Cambridge Ring

Present-day Cambridge Ring LANs are named after the original ring-type LAN developed and installed at Cambridge University's computer centre in the mid-1970s although they differ from this installation in a number of respects.

The original Cambridge Ring LAN was conceived as a solution to the problem of high-speed data transfer between computers and associated equipment within the laboratory. Its success in this role is attested to by the number of commercial manufacturers producing systems based on it.

The original Cambridge Ring LAN was a register-insertion network running at 10MB but this was quickly changed to an empty-slot access system, for practical reasons. Empty-slot rings tend to need less hardware at the node and are less vulnerable to node failures (see Chapter 2 for ring access methods). The network uses a system of dual twisted-pair connections between repeaters, and these cables carry the power for the repeaters as well as the signals. The repeaters can thus continue working if the rest of the node fails. In the network, the sole purpose of the repeater is to boost the incoming signal, allow the node access to the signal as required, and retransmit the signal to the next repeater in the ring with a minimum of delay. All the circuitry concerned with recognising the addresses and emptying or filling the circulating slot are contained in the 'station', which is attached to the repeater. See Fig. 7.4 for a Cambridge Ring node.

When the ring is powered up, a monitor station sets all the initial operating characteristics such as number and type of circulating packets before the normal nodes can operate. Once normal operation is under way, the monitor is used to detect system errors and failures and, where possible, to take corrective action.

The Cambridge Ring data packet is shown in Fig. 7.5. This packet is very short in comparison with equivalent bus LAN packets (see Ethernet

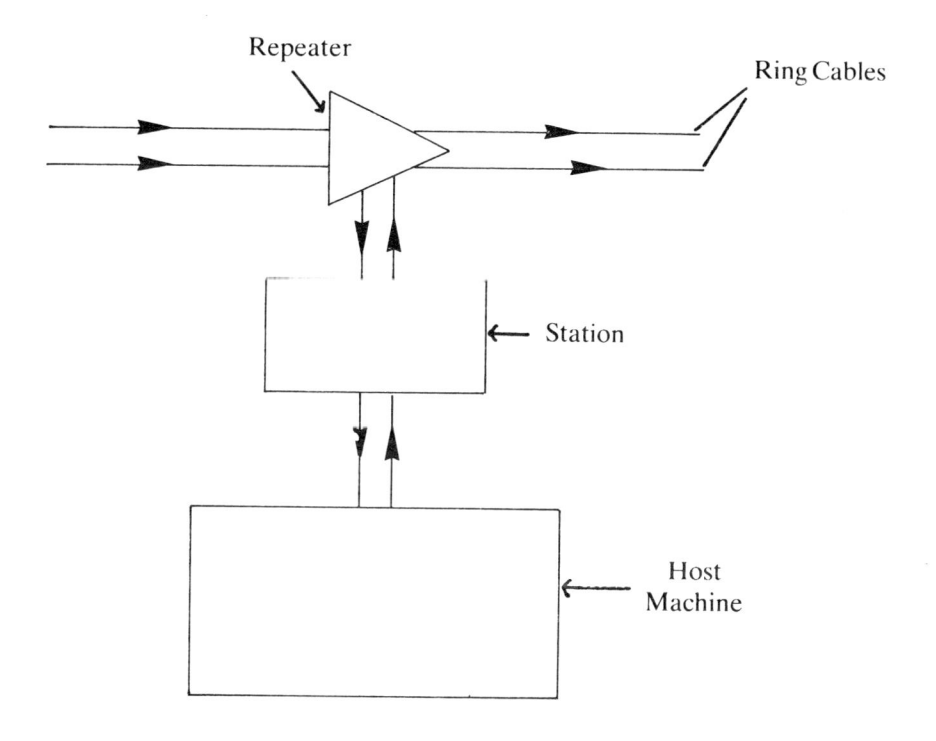

Fig. 7.4 Cambridge Ring node

specification) but this is a constraint of ring-type networks. Perhaps it would be fairer to say that long packets are a constraint of CSMA/CD bus networks, as Cambridge Ring data packets can be lengthened as desired, if the user is prepared to accept a non-standard network. The packet consists of the following items, in order of transmission:

1. Start bit. 1 bit – used to initiate and synchronise the repeater.

2. Full/empty marker. 1 bit – set by the transmitting node and cleared when the packet has been successfully received.

3. Monitor bit. 1 bit – set by the transmitting node and cleared by the monitor as it passes. If the monitor receives a full slot with this bit set to 0, it identifies an error in the system operation and clears the slot to prevent it circulating endlessly.

4. Destination address. 8 bits – one of 256 combinations identifying the receiver node. Address 0 is the monitor, and address 255 is a broadcast address, meaning all nodes should receive the packet.

```
                                            Parity              1 bit
                                            Response            2 bits
                                            Data byte 2         8 bits
                                            Data byte 1         8 bits
                                            Source Address      8 bits
                                            Destination Address 8 bits
                                            Monitor             1 bit
                                            Full/Empty          1 bit
                                            Start               1 bit
```

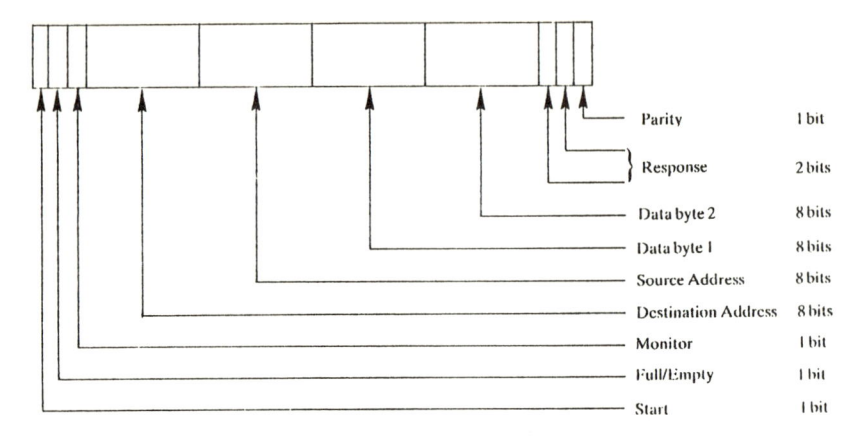

Fig. 7.5 Cambridge Ring data packet.

5. Source address. 8 bits – identifies the transmitting node.

6. Data. 16 bits – the information content of the packet.

7. Response bits. 2 bits – used by the receiving node to pass information back to the transmitting node. Both bits are set by the transmitter and if the packet is successfully received, the first bit is cleared by the receiver and the packet is passed back to the transmitter. If for some reason the packet is not accepted by the receiver, the second bit is cleared instead. This is used if, for example, the packet was garbled in transmission and the parity check has failed. If the receiver is busy i.e. unable to accept the packet, it clears both bits. The transmitter thus has a clear idea of what has happened to the packet when it receives it back and can decide what to do.

8. Parity. 1 bit – a simple parity check bit to determine whether any of the other bits in the packet have been altered in transmission.

The Cambridge Ring network is arranged so that every packet successfully transmitted travels round the ring in its entirety, only being removed by the transmitting node when it is sure that the packet was received correctly. Rogue packets with corrupted addresses or information bits are identified and removed by the monitor station. Note that 'removal' of a packet merely consists of setting the full/empty marker to 'empty' leaving the rest of the contents to continue circulating until the slot is seized by another transmitting node.

To ensure fair usage of slots, a transmitting node cannot immediately re-use a slot it has just emptied, but must pass it on to the next node in line. This ensures that a node with a lot of data to transmit does not prevent other nodes from also using the network.

As the standard Cambridge Ring data packet only contains 2 bytes of data and a simple 1-bit parity check, some means of transferring large amounts of data with sophisticated error checking must be provided if the network is to be used for practical high-speed data transfer. To this end, three high-level protocols for data transfer are available:

1. Basic block protocol. This is the simplest of the three and is made up of a number of the data packets examined above. The information contained in it consists of data about the type of protocol and the length of the block, as well as the 'payload' data, and a checksum to ensure that corruption of data is detected. This protocol is used to do a simple one-way transfer of data.

2. Single-shot protocol. A more complex version of 1., designed for call and response operation, as in most terminal-to-host connections.

3. Byte stream protocol. Based again on the Basic Block protocol, but used to transfer large amounts of data. The Byte Stream protocol is effectively a hard-wired link between transmitting and receiving nodes, allowing data to be transferred rapidly and continuously.

Ethernet and the Cambridge Ring in the future

Both these LANs stand above an ever-proliferating market of non-standard and incompatible networks and this fact along should ensure their continued success. Of the two, Ethernet will undoubtedly find the widest applications, not due to its technical merits, although it has many, but rather due to its widespread support amongst major manufacturers, particularly in the USA. Its only drawbacks are its unsuitability for video transmission and process control, and its expense, which may make it unsuitable for many low-cost applications. The fact that is is now being offered as an integral part of some manufacturers office and computing systems will also enhance its popularity.

The Cambridge Ring is much more of a UK phenomenon, where it has found a home in many universities and research insitutes. Within this environment, its high speed and versatility will ensure its continued popularity but it is less likely to gain commercial acceptance than Ethernet unless it finds a suitable backer with the commerical standing of the Xerox Corporation.

It is likely that both networks will remake themselves in order to conform more closely with the standards promulgated by the ISO and similar bodies. Indeed, this has already started to happen, and will continue until most users' requirements are served by the available technology.

CHAPTER 8
Proprietary LANs

Most of this book has examined the theory behind local area networks and tried to explain what they are, and what they do. This general overview will hopefully be very useful to anyone wishing to install a LAN, as well as anyone desiring a closer understanding of the subject, but an idea of the practical details of real LANs would also be helpful to people in the first category. To this end, a section is included here which gives details of a selection of proprietary LANs covering most areas of interest. The selection has been based on criteria of relative low cost and wide applicability. LANs specific to one manufacturer's equipment have been excluded for this reason, except where the equipment can be regarded as widespread and therefore an industry standard e.g. Acorn/BBC, IBM PC, Apple.

Inclusion in this section should not be taken as a recommendation for the network involved. The information given is taken from, or checked against, the manufacturer's own specifications as far as possible but should not be taken as exhaustive or completely up-to-date, as all manufacturers are continually altering and improving their products.

Econet

Econet is the name of Acorn Computers' low-cost LAN, produced specifically for their own computing equipment. This range presently includes the Acorn Atom, the BBC Microcomputer, and Acorn Systems 3, 4 and 5.

Econet is designed to interconnect these microcomputers and allow them access to shared resources such as file stores and printers.

Because it has been designed for use with Acorn's own products which are relatively inexpensive, Econet is itself less expensive to purchase and install then most of the other networks we will examine. This means that it cannot have the same performance as most LANs and is restricted in speed of operation and versatility compared with Ethernet based LANs, for example, although it bears a resemblance to them physically. Within its chosen field, it provides adequate performance and a full range of functions, including some which are quite unusual but invaluable in an educational context, as we shall see.

Education is one of the main areas where Acorn and BBC microcomputers are found in large concentrations, and this is where Econet has proved extremely successful.

Econet hardware

Econet's general specification is as follows:

Topology	– tree (bus)
Access Method	– CSMA/CD
Transmission	– baseband
Medium	– twin twisted-pair cable
Range	– variable (max. 1km)
Speed	– variable (max. 307KB/s)
No. of nodes	– 256 (including broadcast node)

The specifications indicate that it does not have the same level of performance as some of the networks regarded as standard e.g. Ethernet, despite having initial similarities.

Fig. 8.1 shows a typical Econet system, with a number of workstations using a file server. In addition, it is apparent that this network requires termination boxes at each end of the bus, and a 'clock box' at some point within the system.

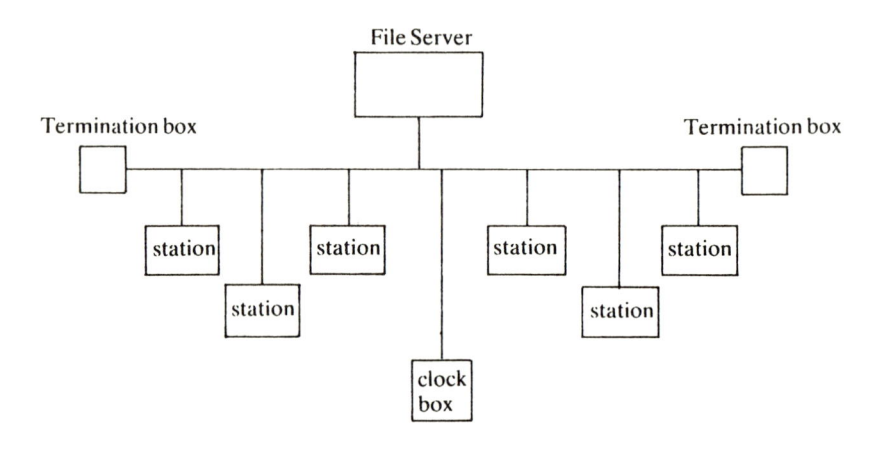

Fig. 8.1 Typical Econet configuration

The terminators at each end of the cable must be provided with 8V power supplies, as must the clock unit.

The bus consists of a cable containing two twisted-pair wires and a shield. This sort of cable is much cheaper than the coaxial cable used in high-capacity LANs. Both ends of the bus must be terminated in standard 5-pin DIN 180° connectors, to which are attached the terminator boxes. Similar connectors are wired into the bus whenever a device is to be attached.

One of the twisted pairs is, obviously, for the transmission of data. The other is used to transmit the clock signal from the clock box to all parts of the system. All devices on the network need this clock and will not function without it. The clock signal is in fact a fixed-frequency square wave which is used to set baud rates and synchronise transmissions, and to achieve the best results, the clock box should be sited close to the centre of the bus.

Econet stations are connected to the bus by a maximum of two metres of twisted-pair cable. Each station must have a unique address within the system and the network will not function if there are two stations with the same address. The address is selected by shorting links on the station's Econet interface card, where eight links are placed in line. A shorted link is a 0, an open one is 1, the group of eight giving a binary representation of the station's address. Addresses 0 and 255 are reserved for broadcast messages i.e. a message sent to address 0 or 255 will be heeded by all stations.

The system clock rate can be selected by switch in the clock box. The chosen clock rate depends on the distance from the clock box of the furthest station, because there is a finite delay in the clock signal travelling along the line to the station. As the distance to the furthest station is increased, the maximum permitted clock rate is proportionally reduced, according to the formula:

Clock Rate = velocity of signal in cable/(distance to furthest station x 4)

For the clock signals available from the Econet clock box, the following max. distances apply when using the recommended cable:

Clock	Distance
307 kHz	100 m.
230 kHz	150 m.
153 kHz	240 m.
115 kHz	330 m.
76 kHz	500 m.

So, the maximum network size and speed quoted at the start of this section are mutually exclusive. This is one of the disadvantages of networks using centralised clocks, rather than having each station generate its own, but in return the cost per node is substantially reduced, as there is then no need for the clock generation circuitry, or the synchronisation circuitry required to identify an incoming asynchronous data signal. Also, the transmitted data does not need to be preceded by a long preamble, such as the one preceding the Ethernet packet, which exists purely for synchronisation purposes. In these circumstances the lower clock rate of a centrally-clocked network may still allow an equal amount of useful data to be transmitted in a given time.

Econet software

Econet software offers three main facilities. These are: access to a file server, access to a printer server, and access to other user stations. The first two are fairly standard for most LANs, but Econet's implementation of the third facility allows some unusual functions, which are unique and very suitable for educational purposes.

1. File Server. The file server is a program resident in a station on the network. The station must control a disc system which is used for file storage. Users call this station, which has address 254, to store or retrieve programs and data from the disc system, which then appears to each station as if it were directly attached to them. All the normal functions of a disc file system are available, including listing of disc contents by filename (CAT), information about a file (INFO), deletion of unwanted files (DELETE), renaming (RENAME), and a means of preventing unauthorised access to, and alteration of, files (ACCESS). This last function allows a user to prevent other users reading from, writing to, or deleting one of his files, depending on the way the command is used. It also allows a user to safeguard against accidental alteration or deletion of his own files, where necessary.

The file structure is heirarchical – that is to say, any file can be a list of other files, which can only be reached through that file. Each of these sub-files can in turn be a list, or directory, of further files – and so on. This type if file system is a very efficient method of organising data, as files with something in common can be grouped under a single directory. However, a heirarchical file system is also a good place to lose data, if care is not taken.

In order to use the file server, a user must log on, i.e. identify himself to the file server by giving it a username. This name forms the directory name under which all that user's files are grouped.

2. The printer server. This is a program resident in a station on the network which receives data and programs from other stations and prints them on its attached printer. One printer can, therefore, be used to service the needs of the whole network. The printer server normally has address 235 on the network, although this can be altered if desired. Once a station has contacted the printer server and started to use it, other stations on the network are unable to contact the printer server until the first station releases it.

3. Other stations. It is normal for a network to provide some means of interstation communication. Econet's educational bias has resulted in an emphasis on screen transfer, rather than file transfer. The VIEW program, loaded from the file server, allows a user to copy another station's screen onto his own for examination. Using VIEW within a continuous program loop allows the screen to be constantly updated with the remote screen's information, effectively making the user's screen a slave to the remote screen. The user's keyboard remains active throughout this process.

Another program useful for teaching is REMOTE, which allows a user to take over another station, so that anything typed on the user's machine is executed on the remote station's machine. Also, everything written to the remote screen is written to the user's screen and the remote keyboard is disabled.

Econet also provides a message function, called NOTIFY, which allows text to be sent to another station, appearing on that station's screen.

Clearway

Clearway is a low-cost general-purpose LAN, produced by Real Time Developments Ltd of Farnborough, Hants. It is designed to alleviate the problems caused in offices and laboratories when incompatible equipment is purchased individually. Most computer users are familiar with the difficulties caused when communication ports in personal computers and peripherals will not operate together, or when connecting leads have to be changed with monotonous regularity as different configurations of equipment are required. Clearway does away with these difficulties by connecting a data ring to the RS232C serial port on each device. By using the RS232C port, which nearly all small computers and peripherals have, Clearway sidesteps two problems:

1. Restriction to a limited range of devices with suitable Input/Output facilities, and

2. The need to install a LAN interface within the device.

RS232C is an industry standard for serial data communication and virtually all computer manufacturers provide some version of it within their equipment. It is, however, a standard encompassing many minor variations and reduced versions. It does not, for example, define the data transmission speed of the data link, and it allows a wide variety of data formats and control signals under its umbrella. These variables are the normal stumbling blocks when setting up a serial data link between two ostensibly compatible devices. The Clearway node is set up to match the RS232C idiosyncrasies of its attached device, and converts the data it receives into a standard form for transmission on the LAN.

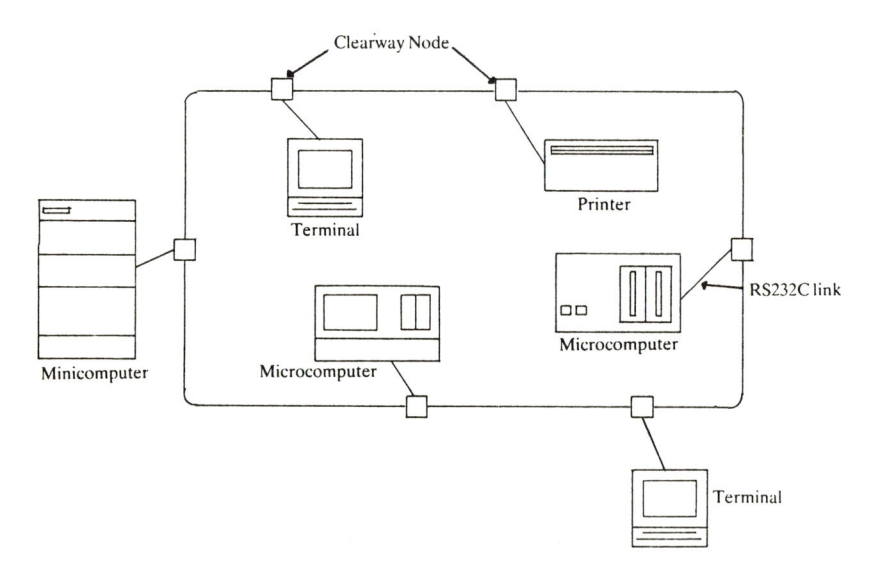

Fig. 8.2 Typical Clearway system

The technical specification for Clearway is as follows:

Topology   – ring
Access method   – register insertion
Transmission   – baseband
Medium   – 75 Ohm coaxial cable
Range   – 800m between nodes without repeaters
Speed   – 56 KB/s
No. of nodes   – 99

Clearway hardware

Clearway is a ring-based LAN and has many characteristics in common with the more expensive high-speed rings. Each node is a separate, powered unit which receives and passes on ring transmissions, and inserts or removes data relevant to the node. The user transfers data to and from the Clearway unit via the RS232C link. However, in keeping with its low-cost, technically-straightforward attitude, the Clearway hardware does away with some of the usual ring problems. The connecting cable is 75 Ohm coaxial cable – normal TV aerial cable, which is relatively cheap. Also, the repeaters within each node are not powered from the ring, but from each Clearway unit's power supply. If a node loses power, a relay switches the node repeater out of the ring, thus ensuring that the data ring is unbroken despite the failure of one node.

In fact, any number of nodes can be switched off as long as the distance between powered nodes does not exceed 800m. These provisions make Clearway an extremely robust network which avoids many of the inherent difficulties of ring LANs.

Each Clearway network unit has a jack socket for ring data in, and a lead terminated in a jack plug for ring data out. This can be plugged directly into the next Clearway unit socket, or into an extended ring socket.

If the Clearway network is used in a small area, it is possible to connect a complete ring without any extra cables or components.

The unit is mains-powered, and has a mains lead attached. The only other connection is the 25-way D-type socket for the RS232C connection to the attached device. This RS232C connection provides for a variety of control lines, which the Clearway unit can be programmed to provide or respond to. Briefly, Clearway can cope with the following RS232C variation:

Baud rate	– 50 – 9600 baud
Handshaking	– software: XON/XOFF; hardware: DTR/CTS; lines: none
Parity	– odd, even, mark, space or none
Character size	– 7 or 8 bit

These variables cover the commonly used formats for serial data transmission over RS232C links, allowing Clearway to accommodate most if not all terminals, printers and microcomputers.

The Clearway units have error indications, either in the form of a Light Emitting Diode (LED), or a Liquid Crystal Display (LCD), which inform the user when anything goes wrong, and also what operation is being carried out during normal functioning.

Clearway also provides variations on the standard nodes to suit certain needs. There is a rack-mounting system which can take up to ten nodes, allowing them to be physically grouped together, and two multiplexing nodes. The model 'B' is a byte multiplexing node which allows a number of nodes access to it at the same time. The data bytes coming in are sorted by the model 'B' and presented to the single RS232 connection. This will normally be attached to a computer which has the facilities to separate the various incoming bytes and identify them correctly. The process also works in reverse, with the computer attached to the model 'B' node transmitting to several other nodes simultaneously. The model 'M' node is a message-multiplexing unit, which receives messages from various nodes and presents them to the RS232C output, after sorting. It is a variation of the model 'B', differing chiefly in the way it handles data.

Clearway software

Since Clearway is a stand-alone general-purpose LAN, which only requires a standard serial data link from its users, there is no software supplied as standard for tasks such as file transfer. However, Clearway do supply the Peachtree Telecommunications software for CP/M and MSDOS-based microcomputer systems.

This lack of software is not a serious problem in Clearway's main area of operations, which is the setting-up of virtual circuits between different types of devices. Large numbers of similar devices e.g. IBM PCs which all require a single filing or printing service would be better off with a LAN tailored to their own characteristics. A general-purpose LAN covering these functions would, as Clearway point out, be considerably more expensive.

Clearway's software content consists of the programming contained within each node, which configures the node when it is switched on, and then allows the user to set up all the conditions necessary for it to communicate effectively with whatever is plugged in to the RS232C socket.

To set up a node, the user simply connects a terminal to it and presses the reset button on the node. The terminal will display a line of text from the node, containing the following data:

1. A 2-digit number representing the address of the remote node your local node is connected to.

2. A '*' if the Clearway connection is not to be broken after it has been idle for more than 30sec. Any other character for a 30sec. timeout.

3. A single digit representing the baud rate of the RS232C link from the attached device.

4. A single character designating the handshaking method employed by the device attached to the local node.

5. A single character designating the type of parity required by the device plugged into the RS232C connections.

6. A single digit representing the baud rate of the Clearway unit to the attached device.

7. A single character designating the type of handshaking to be employed by the Clearway unit.

8. A 2-digit number representing the address of the node to which the Clearway unit is connected. The value must be unique and greater than 00.

9. A single character which will be recognised in future by the Clearway unit as the signal to enter set-up mode. This avoids having to press the reset button to change settings.

10. Space for free text to provide messages.

11. A representation of the node error status.

If the information displayed is satisfactory the user types 'Y' and the system starts operation. If anything needs to be altered, the user types 'N' and can then reset any parameter as desired before operating the node. After the node has been set up for the first time, the only change normally required will be a change of destination address.

As the system is described so far, only pairs of devices can be linked together, excluding the possibility of more than one device transmitting to a single receiver. This is obviously not satisfactory where, for example, a number of microcomputers need the services of a single printer. To avoid this, Clearway has a 'fictitious' remote address, 00. Entering this value in the remote node space allows the local node to receive from any source. However, once a device is transmitting to this local node, no other device can butt in until the transmission has stopped for 30 sec., thus ensuring the continuity of the virtual data circuit during a transmission. Any number of nodes can be set up in this way.

Clearway is transparent to the user in operation, fulfilling all the requirements of a local area network, and trading high-speed and software support for general applicability and low cost. It is likely to be a much more practical solution to the problems of the small computer user than a true Cambridge Ring type network.

Multilink

Multilink is a low-cost local area network system produced by Nine Tiles Computer Systems Ltd of Cambridge. Multilink is designed to link terminals, peripherals and computers together to form a reliable, cost-effective and integrated system. It has been conceived from the start as a network for microcomputers and similar devices and its features reflect this. Like most of the networks featured in this section, Multilink can be a "second-stage" addition to a computing system, introduced after the initial purchase of microcomputers and peripherals are already in action. To this end, it provides interfaces for most popular microcomputer hardware and software.

Multilink is also supplied under licence by Hawker Siddeley Dynamics Engineering Ltd. As well as board-level network interfaces and software, Multilink integrated circuits are available to manufacturers, who can then build Multilink directly into the microcomputers and peripherals they manufacture.

Multilink has the following characteristics:

Topology	– ring
Access method	– buffer insertion (register insertion)
Transmission	– baseband
Medium	– twisted-pair cable
Range	– 1 km between active nodes
Speed	– 250 KB/s
No. of nodes	– 125

From this, it can be seen that Multilink bears some resemblance to other low-cost networks, but certain design features make it worthy of individual attention, as we shall observe.

Multilink hardware

Multilink is unusual amongst low-cost networks in offering a wide range of network interface units. Most LANs in this area only have one standard connection to the network, either in the form of a universal interface e.g. Clearway's RS232C connection, or in the form of a printed circuit board which plugs into a specific type of device, e.g. IBM's PC Net. In the latter case, use of other equipment on the network requires one of the standard nodes as an interface unit. In other words, a PC or Apple will be tied up purely as a file server, or printer server, and be prevented from doing any other work.

Multilink offers three different types of network interface: stand-alone stations, which provide general-purpose RS232C connections; computer interface cards, which provide a specific plug-in interface for a number of different microcomputers; and chip sets, which are the central part of the

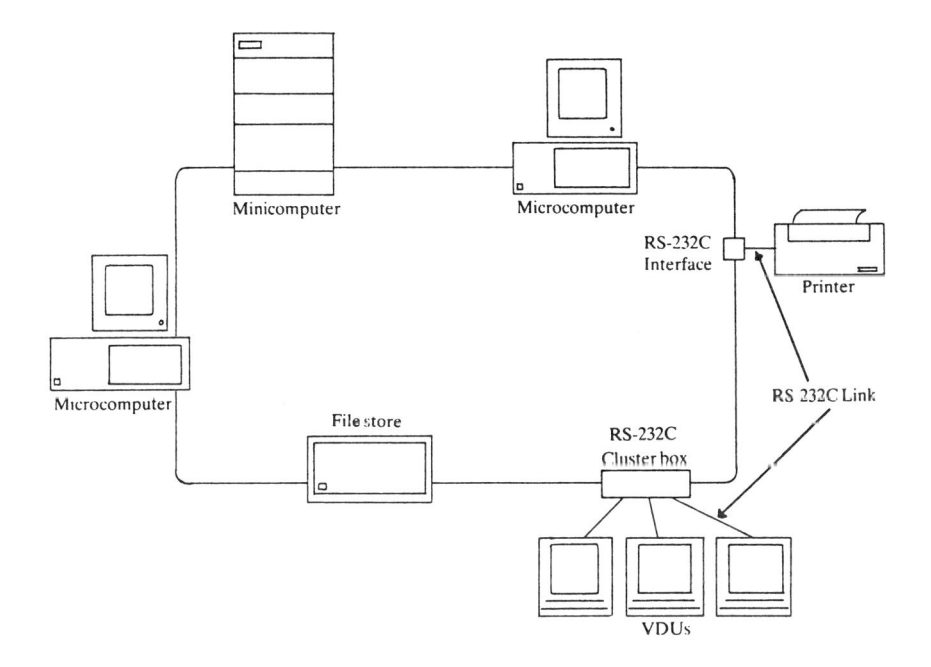

Fig. 8.3 Typical Multilink system

other two types of interface but are available separately to allow users and manufacturers to build their own interfaces. All three types of interface can be mixed together in any combination within a network as the network node portion of each unit is identical.

The stand-alone stations provide one, four, or eight RS232C ports on one network node. The ports have selectable baud rates and data formats. Hardware and software flow controls are provided, allowing the ports to connect to virtually all RS232C devices. The parameters for operation can be selected by software, allowing attached devices to reconfigure the ports as necessary.

Plug-in interface cards are available for the following microcomputers and bus systems:

    IBM PC and compatibles
    Apricot
    Apple IIe and II
    BBC model B
    Epson QX10 and QX16
    Wren

Kaypro
Olivetti
DEC Unibus (acts as DZII interface)
DEC LSI-II (Q-bus)
S100 Bus
Intel Multibus

Some of these interfaces are designed to be used with the SimpleNet software supplied by Nine Tiles to operate Multilink. Others are meant to be used without any extra software e.g. BBC 'B' interface, which comes with a plug-in ROM providing a network filing system and other usual network facilities. The great advantage of these plug-in interfaces is that they connect directly to the attached device, rather than through a serial link, and they can operate at much higher speeds becasue of this direct access.

Also available is a range of filestores, designed to act as file servers in a Multilink system. These consist of hard disk units varying in size from 10 to 40 Mbytes, with optional 60Mbyte tape cartridge unit. The tape cartridge unit is available separately. The units contain SimpleNet fileserver software in ROM, and a clock-calendar facility.

Multilink stand-alone stations are mains-powered, and plug-in interfaces are powered by the attached device. In order to ensure the integrity of the ring when the device or station is switched off, a relay is included to bypass the node when it is unpowered. So, as long as the distance between powered nodes does not exceed the 1km limit, any number of nodes in a Multilink network can be left out of operation.

Data transmission along the network cable closely resembles RS422 (V.11) transmission standards i.e. differential mode transmission and while twisted-pair cable is recommended, reasonable results should be obtained over short distances with other types of cable e.g. mains cable.

Data transmitted on the ring appears in the form shown in Fig. 8.4. The first part of the data packet is the 'header' which contains source and destination addresses for the data, and a character count. Following this comes the data itself. The number of bytes is variable and is decided by the Multilink node depending on such factors as ring availability, device speed etc. The range is 1 to 85 bytes, plus the header and the trailer, which contains a checksum for the packet. In general, the packet size will be greater for faster devices.

In operation, a node wishing to transmit monitors the ring and, on detecting a gap between packets, starts transmission of its own packet. Any data arriving during this time is diverted to a buffer and held until the outgoing

```
┌─────────┬──────┬─────────┐
│ HEADER  │ DATA │ TRAILER │
└─────────┴──────┴─────────┘
```

Contains checksum

Data: 1 to 85 bytes

Source address,
Destination Address,
and Character count

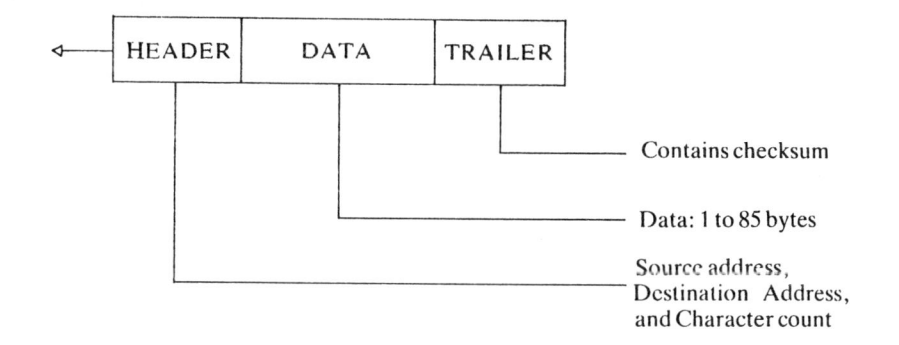

Fig. 8.4 Multilink packet structure

packet has finished. The incoming packet is then retransmitted. For more detail on buffer and register insertion, see Chapter 2.

Multilink software

Operating software for Multilink is in two parts: the Disc-based Simplenet set of programs which allow microcomputers and similar devices to use the network to its full extent, and the software contained in ROM within the stand-alone stations.

Simplenet is a software package which runs under the control of a microcomputer operating system and is designed to allow the user to have access to the whole network, which appears to him as a large heirarchical file system. Transmitting data across the network is thus made to look like file transfers within a single system. Simplenet is available for MS-DOS, PC-DOS, CP/M and UNIX operating systems, which covers virtually all popular microcomputers and a large number of scientific minicomputers.

The software in the stand-alone stations sees the attached device as either interactive (VDU, etc.), multiplexed (multi-access computer) or standard. The distinction is important for such things as error messages. The attached device can specify operating parameters to the Multilink station. These include:

>Type of attached device
>Data flow control (XON/XOFF, DTR/CTS)
>Character on line operation
>Echo mode
>Baud rate of attached device
>Character size and parity

The user supplies an identification for the Multilink station which can be up to 15 characters long. Alternatively, stations can be identified by their relative position on the ring. A series of simple commands are available to perform network functions such as Set Identifier, Connect to another node, Program a remote node, Set options for station, and others. These commands are input by the attached device, either directly by the user in the case of a VDU, or under software control in the case of a microcomputer.

Multilink has a number of diagnostic features which help to ensure efficient operation, and in the case of faults, to ensure detection of the problem. As with nearly all LANs, receipt of a data packet is acknowledged by the destination node on the network. The acknowledgment packet either indicates correct reception or receipt of a packet containing checksum errors. In the latter case, the source node transmits the original packet again. The transmitting node will report a failure if a packet is not received correctly after a certain number of re-transmissions.

If no acknowledgment to a packet is received, Multilink suspects a break in the ring and reports this, together with an indication of the relative position of the break in the ring.

Where a packet containing an invalid destination address occurs, Multilink will not allow it to circulate the ring indefinitely – all packets are removed after passing through a certain number of nodes. If there is no traffic on the network for a time, each node will transmit to itself to test for a break in the ring and report the results of its test.

V-Net

V-Net is described as a low-cost machine-independent local area network and is supplied by Format PC of Belper, Derbyshire.

Like many low-cost LANs, V-Net uses the RS232 serial port available on most microcomputers and peripherals to connect devices to the network. It differs, however, in one respect because its topology is fairly unusual for low-cost networks. The network nodes are connected in a star configuration, with the RS232 cables forming the arms of the star. These plug into a central unit which provides the true networking facilities, interconnecting the various stations on demand.

V-Net bears some resemblance to the PABXs discussed earlier, with its star configuration and central switching facility, but it is a true network designed purely for serial digital data.

V-Net hardware

V-Net has the following characteristics:

Topology	– star
Access Method	– time division multiplex
Transmission	– baseband
Medium	– RS232 serial link (externally)
Range	– RS232 standard
Speed	– maximum 9600 baud per node
No. of nodes	– 32

The V-Net system consists of the central V-Net 'stack' and attached devices. All the hard work of the system is carried out within the stack which comprises a power supply unit, the V-Net bus controller, and a number of RS232 ports. The power supply unit is there to power the bus controller and the RS232 ports. The V-Net Bus Controller regulates interconnection and data transfer between the installed RS232 ports on the stack, giving all the ports an equal time period in which to transfer data to its destination port. This time division arrangment allows the system to function at maximum speed for each link (9600 baud) regardless of the number of people using the system, and the load each user is imposing on the network. V-Net thus has a guaranteed maximum access time, which may be important in some applications.

The RS232 ports come in four-port units, which plug onto the V-Net stack one on top of another. The maximum number on a single stack is eight units, which gives a total of 32 ports. A minimum V-Net system consists of the power supply, bus controller, and one 4-way RS232 port unit. V-Net, therefore, allows a network to consist of 4 to 32 nodes, in steps of 4. The stack contains *all* the network except the cabling and is a very compact unit.

The RS232 ports are individually configurable for baud rate, parity, number of stop bits, and handshaking protocol – either hardware (DTS/CTS) or software (XON/XOFF). To cope with different transmit and receive baud rates, each V-Net port has its own 2K byte character output buffer.

V-Net ports are identified within the network by a 2-digit address. The first digit is the position of the port's unit in the stack, and the second is the port's position within the unit. Thus the first digit of an address can be 1 to 8, but the second can only be 1 to 4. When this number is transmitted to the stack from a node wishing to establish contact, V-Net responds with a message stating that the channel is open, engaged, or unobtainable. If the channel is open, data can be transferred between the two attached devices without any problems of mismatched baudrates or parity, as these are adjusted automatically by V-Net.

If the address requested is engaged, V-Net has a facility which can automatically reroute the connection to another address, allowing the user to connect to an alternative printer for example. This feature is particularly useful where a number of devices regularly need to communicate with a particular service.

To terminate a connection, either of the attached devices must transmit a character to the stack. This character can be either control Y or break and is selectable independently for each port.

This is the standard V-Net system. To make greater use of it, various enhancements are available including an RS422 cable extension which allows the link to cover a much greater distance than the standard RS232 connection, but appears as an RS232 connection to each end. This is done by building RS232-422 convertors into both ends of the cable which are powered directly from the V-Net stack. There is also a 64K byte printer buffer which sists in line with the system printer or plotter, allowing a user to dump data to the buffer rapidly and go on to other things while the printer continues working.

Gateways to other standard networks such as Ethernet and Cambridge Ring are also available.

V-Net software

To make the best use of the network, V-Net can supply a central fileserver to allow file transfer and storage. The unit consists of a hard disc with an optional tape cartridge backup. the disc is available in several different sizes.

Files are stored in the file server in a common format, regardless of the type of device on which they originated. This will allow files to be transferred between dissimilar devices with the same operating system, and will allow ASCII files to be transferred throughout the system.

V-Net also supply software for most of the microcomputers likely to be connected to the network. The software package allows users to operate V-Net by means of simple commands displayed on a menu. The functions available include:

1. File transfer: files may be transferred to and from other connected microcomputers and the fileserver if one is installed.

2. Assign printer: a user can select either a printer connected locally to the microcomputer or remotely via the network. All print commands issued by the user will be directed by the software to whichever printer has been selected.

3. Terminal mode: the microcomputer can be operated as a terminal to a remote host computer via V-Net. This allows a user to access more powerful devices and work with them directly if necesary reverting to local operation when it is suitable.

Since the software is available for all popular types of PCs and microcomputers which have disc drives, and runs under all the main disc operating systems, V-Net can be used to interconnect virtually any combination of devices, making it very suitable as an 'add-on' network for installations which already have a wide variety of equipment in use.

IBM PC networks

IBM currently supplies two networking products for its range of PCs which come under the heading of low-cost LANs. A large number of other manufacturers supply LANs specifically aimed at the IBM PC market but in this section we will look solely at those networks supplied by IBM for IBM equipment, in order to give some idea of IBM's own attitudes towards LANs in relation to their PC range.

The two networks offered by IBM are referred to as the PC Cluster and the PC Network. They are designed to cover two ranges of network functions with the PC Cluster being the simpler, less sophisticated system. It offers the standard functions required by users of small networks and is likely to be the one chosen by first-time network users who wish to expand the uses of a small group of PCs.

The PC Network is a more sophisticated and extensive system which can provide comprehensive resource sharing of files, printers, data and programs, plus an electronic messaging system.

A comparison of the specifications of the two systems highlights the differences effectively. The PC Cluster is as follows:

Topology	– bus
Access method	– CSMA/CD
Transmission	– baseband
Medium	– 75 ohm coaxial cable
Range	– 1000 m

Speed   – 375K bits/sec
No. of nodes   – 64

whereas the PC Network has the following specification:

Topology   – tree
Access method   – CSMA/CD
Transmission   – broadband
Medium   – 75 ohm coaxial cable
Range   – 304.8m to translator unit 609.6m between nodes
Speed   – 2 Mbits/sec
No. of nodes   – 72

The two systems share the same transmission medium but use it in different ways. As we have seen, broadband transmission of data allows much greater flexibility of network use, and much greater capacity for traffic within the network, but is normally more expensive to install. The transmission speed of the PC Network is approximately six times that of the PC Cluster which added to its broadband capability, make the PC Network a different class of system from the cluster.

As both networks are designed purely for the IBM PC range, connection to the PC is made by plugging adaptor cards directly into the PC system. This does away with the necessity of converting the data to be transmitted on the network into RS232 form, or similar, and thus cuts down on the amount of hardware in the connection. It also frees the available RS232 ports for other tasks.

Software must also be tailored specifically for the computer and network, and must be installed in all the devices in the system which means that, as the two networks stand, any shared resource such as a printer or disc store must be connected to the network through an IBM PC. However, the PC Network has many expansion possibilities and is likely to have a variety of third-party hardware available when it has been adopted by sufficient users. IBM's established user base and reputation will ensure the success of both networks.

IBM PC Cluster

We will now examine the hardware and software involved in the IBM PC Cluster in more detail.

The PC Cluster is designed to provide the following functions:

1. Use of a single system with a hard disc to serve all other stations in a cluster.

2. Use of space on a share disc as a public volume, used by all stations in the cluster to share programs and read-only information.

3. Use of space on a shared disc as private read/write volumes, one for each station in the cluster.

4. Sending and receiving messages station-to-station within the cluster.

5. Transfer of files station-to-station within the cluster.

Remote stations can perform initial program load using programs held on the disc server.

The PC Cluster program and its associated hardware is designed to allow a group of PCs to be linked together as a working group, with each unit enjoying the facilities of all the other units in the cluster. A single PCXT or PC with expansion unit can provide a central filing service for all the PCs in the cluster.

The minimum hardware requirements are that each IBM PC (including XTs, ATs and Portables) in the Cluster must have one diskette drive, 128Kb of memory (256Kb in the case of the disc server), an IBM PC Cluster Adapter, Version 2.10 of the PC Disk Operating System and an 80-column display with appropriate adapter.

If the Cluster does not utilise a disc server, at least one of the stations in the cluster must have a double-sided diskette drive.

The PC Cluster is obviously designed as a low-cost entry into the networking field for users of IBM PCs. Although the system allows a maximum of 64 nodes, it is unlikely that anything like that number will be connected or used. IBM state that performance may be affected as units are added to the cluster, as one might expect of a baseband CSMA/CD network with a low data rate (only 375Kb per second). It is likely that the PC Cluster will find most of its applications in offices and laboratories where a small number of PCs are used to perform similar tasks in a limited area, and where the simple resource sharing offered by the PC Cluster will prevent duplications of hardware and software.

IBM PC Network

The IBM PC Network is described by IBM as a low-cost, high function broadband LAN for the family of IBM PCs. The term low-cost is, as we have seen, a relative thing, and the PC Network is certainly more expensive than the PC Cluster described previously. It does however offer a great deal more in terms of speed and functions. The basic functions it provides are similar to those of the PC Cluster i.e. print serving, file serving, file transfer and program sharing, and electronic messaging, but the scope of each of these functions is greatly expanded. For example, any station with a hard disc can be a file server and can support up to 32 concurrent user identity codes. In addition, the PC Network can provide electronic mail facilities for messaging and file transfer. When using the system for message management, a single workstation can provide support for 12 user identity codes.

The area covered by the PC Network seems to be less than that covered by the PC Cluster, with the first allowing 609.6m. maximum between two nodes, and the second allowing a full 1000m. However, the 1000m allowed for the PC Cluster is the total length of the bus cable, and every node on the system must be contained within this run of cable. One kilometre sounds a great deal but can quickly be used up in modern office buildings.

The PC Network is a 'tree' network and is in effect a star shape with further stars based on the end of each cable run. The important distance with this topology is the maximum spacing between a node and the central point of the main star. In the PC Network, the central point is the fixed-frequency translator unit and the maximum distance between any node and this unit is 304.8m. Doubling this gives the maximum distance allowed between two nodes. However, the standard translator unit has an 8-way cable splitter and thus the main star can have eight arms, each of which can be 304.8 metres long. In this way, the network can cover a much greater area than the PC Cluster's bus.

The PC Network, as standard, is a versatile LAN, but the configuration allows further expansion without difficulty. Third-party suppliers can provide expansions for up to 255 nodes, and enhanced translator units, also referred to as 'headends', to allow a further 1000 nodes.

The network software also allows expansion of facilities, and users can program their own additional features if required. Because the method of transmission is broadband, other signals as well as the PC Network data can be transmitted. Extra channels of digital data, video signals, and voice signals can all be accommodated in the PC Network, where suitable modems and translator units are provided, making the PC Network suitable for a fully integrated office automation network.

Hardware for the PC Network consists of a plug-in adapter card for each PC on the network, a fixed-frequency translator unit with cable splitter, coaxial cables, and an 8-way base expander. The comprehensive operating and installation software comes in diskette form and requires PC Disc Operating System Version 3.1 to run on a PC.

The IBM PC Network will be attractive to organisations using a large number of IBM PCs as personal workstations, where the improved facilities and shared resources will rapidly repay the cost of installation.

AppleTalk

AppleTalk is Apple Computer's low-cost entry in the microcomputer LAN stakes. It is designed initially to operate with the Apple Macintosh range and Apple have taken the idea of low-cost networking seriously enough to include all the necessary hardware and software as standard in the Macintosh. This means that the extra requirements for turning a Macintosh into an AppleTalk node consist solely of cabling and connectors. The Apple LaserWriter printer also has an AppleTalk interface, making a distributed computing system with a central print server possible without difficulty, simply by plugging the computers and printer together. At present, AppleTalk is available only for Apple equipment, but Apple have made a point of publishing all the technical information about AppleTalk to encourage third party suppliers to develop applications for the LAN. A number of manufacturers have already started work on interfaces for the Apple II and IBM PC, amongst others. Other developments in progress include file servers, electronic mail, print spoolers, and gateways to other networks, including Ethernet and the IBM network.

In the light of these developments, it is possible that AppleTalk could become one of the most widespread PC networks. It will certainly find favour with Apple users who wish to mix Macintoshes with older Apple IIs.

AppleTalk has the following specifications:

Topology	– serial bus
Access method	– CSMA/CA (collision avoidance)
Transmission	– baseband
Medium	– shielded twisted-pair cable
Range	– 300m
Speed	– 230.4 Kbaud
No. of nodes	– 32 max.

It has been designed for use in small work groups where Apple claim 80% of business communication takes place. By limiting the maximum number of nodes to 32, and the transmission speed to 230 Kbaud, the network's designers have simplified the tasks that the software and hardware must carry out. The access method, CSMA/CA, is explained in Chapter 2 and is fairly uncommon in practice. The advantage of collision avoidance (CA) over collision detection (CD) is that the network can be used more efficiently because no time is lost in simultaneous transmissions from two nodes which must be halted on detection and then retransmitted after a random delay. When the bus is clear, a node wishing to transmit, reserves the bus by a brief 'handshake' signal. This prevents other devices from transmitting and the node can then continue uninterrupted.

With these features, the network performance can be optimised to make better use of the available transmission speed, allowing AppleTalk to work as quickly as other networks with higher specifications.

Hardware for AppleTalk consists solely of the AppleTalk connector and a length of twisted-pair cable – everything else is already installed in the Macintosh. Given Apple's predominance in American educational areas, it is likely that AppleTalk will also succeed there.

Infaplug

Infaplug is a local area network produced by Infa Communications Ltd of Taunton. It is designed as a low-cost method of interconnecting large numbers of computers and communicating terminals and, like a number of other systems we have examined, uses the RS232C serial connection in order to connect as many different types and makes of equipment as possible. Infaplug is notable for the positioning of the network electronics, nearly all of which are squeezed into a plug head measuring 115mm x 82mm x 38mm. The plug head has a flying-lead RS232C connection to the equipment and plugs into a wall socket containing the data ring access point. This arrangement makes Infaplug one of the physically smallest non machine-specific networks and these two points, together with its low-cost per node, make it an attractive possibility for installations with a mix of equipment.

The Infaplug specification is as follows:

Topology	– ring
Access method	– not available
Transmission mode	– baseband
Medium	– coaxial cable
Range	– between active Infaplugs:
	a) 800m. if using 75ohm coaxial cable
	b) 400m. if using 320pF/m single core cable
Speed	– 115K bits/s
No. of Nodes	– 255

Infaplug hardware

The Infaplug local area network comprises two parts. One is the Infaplug itself, together with its RS232C connection – this can be regarded as a network node – and the other is the data ring to which the Infaplug connects. The data ring consists of cabling, two or more wall sockets, and one or more ring power units.

The data ring cable can be cheap, telecom-style communication cable for small installations, or coaxial cable for systems covering larger areas. The wall sockets, as well as connecting the Infaplug to the cable, contain circuitry to detect an Infaplug failure. When this occurs, the wall socket disconnects the Infaplug from the ring and will not reconnect it until it has successfully completed a self-test routine. The sockets are cheap as they contain very little active circuitry, and there is no restriction on either the number installed, or their positioning.

The ring power unit is essential as it is the only source of power in the system. All wall sockets and Infaplugs take their supply from it. The ring power unit is run from the mains supply (220 240V or 110V) and provides 30V DC at a maximum of 4A to the ring. This is sufficient to power a maximum of 40 active Infaplugs. If the system needs more than this number of active nodes, a second ring power unit can be incorporated in the network, powering a further 40 Infaplugs. This can be repeated up to the maximum of 255 Infaplugs per network.

The Infaplug comes with a two metre cable terminated in a 25 way D-type connector, the standard for RS232C connections. The RS232C interface can be configured to cover most normal requirements as follows:

Baud rate – 75, 110, 300, 600, 1200, 2400, 4800 and 9600 baud.
   Full duplex with split transmit and receive rates if required.

Handshaking – either: 1) None
             2) Software (XON/XOFF)
             3) Hardware

These features allow the Infaplug to connect to virtually any terminal printer or computer with an RS232C interface and the split baud rates also allow modem connections.

The Infaplug has sophisticated transmission protocols built in, making the network resistant to corruption of data during transmission. If data is received in corrupted form, the transmitting Infaplug automatically re-transmits to ensure that only correct data is passed on.

Infaplug software

Software for the Infaplug network is available at two levels; as well as the embedded operating software within each Infaplug, there is a software package called Infalink which is available for most popular personal computers, allowing them to perform file transfers and control printers.

Using the embedded operating software, links between nodes can be set up by transmitting simple commands along the RS232C link to the Infaplug. Where a VDU or similar is attached to the Infaplug, typing the 'connect' command followed by the name of the other node will set up the link.

Where a computer needs to set up a link, it must also provide the 'connect' command followed by the address of the destination, either through its operating software or by an input from the user. Clearing or disconnecting the link is done in a similar manner.

So, if Infaplug is used in this manner, operation is very simple and straightforward. However, it may be necessary to perform more complicated procedures such as file transfer or print spooling. In these situations the Infalink software package is available to simplify the task of setting up the link and supervising the transfer.

The commands available with Infalink include **ATTACH, SEND, RECV, DIS** and **INFA**.

> **ATTACH** performs the same function as the Connect command direct to the Infaplug, setting up a link between two nodes in the network.
>
> **SEND** transmits the named file from the user's computer to the device at the other end of the link.
>
> **RECV** transmits the named file from the computer at the other end of the link to the user's computer.
>
> **DIS** disconnects the link between the two devices.
>
> **INFA** is used to talk directly to the Infaplug at the user's node, allowing the user to alter the Infaplug's variable parameters such as plug name, baud rate, parity and handshake method.

To use a printer for hard copy, the user simply types **ATTACH** followed by the printer node's name, and then uses the computer's normal printing program to transmit to the printer. While this process is happening, no other device can take control of the printer and must wait until the user types **DIS** at the end of the print.

Infalink is available for nearly all microcomputers running the PCDOS, MSDOS and CPM86 operating systems, making it suitable for most normal office and laboratory applications.

The Infaplug local area network together with the Infalink software are a cost-effective solution to networking problems where low installation costs and compatibility across a wide range of machines are more important then high speed operations.

Commodore Keynet

Keynet is Commodore's own local area network designed to link up to 250 assorted Commodore computers and peripherals together. Its use is restricted to Commodore equipment but it is worthy of inclusion for the same reason as Econet or the IBM networks i.e. the large number of Commodore computers already in use throughout this country and the world.

With so many Commodore machines in use for business purposes, one obvious use for Keynet is in offices and stores for distributed record keeping. The hard disc units available can be used to make one unit on the network a file server for the rest of the network, giving all users the benefit of permanent storage facilities with fast access.

Keynet hardware

With Keynet, one computer is the 'master' system and the others are the 'slaves'. Any computer can be the master as the network interface consists of a printed circuit board which plugs into the computer. Differences between master and slave are contained within the operating firmware and in the switch settings on the printed circuit board.

The network has the following characteristics:

Topology	– bus
Access method	– master/slave pseudo-poll and select
Transmission	– baseband
Medium	– 4 twisted-pairs
Range	– over 1 km
Speed	– 250k baud
Max. no of nodes	– 250 max.

The access method is unusual and has the advantage of requiring little intelligence in the slave units, thus cutting down on memory costs. This is at the expense of depending on one unit – the master – to control the whole network. If the master unit is out of action for any reason, the network will not function.

The following Commodore computers can be connected to Keynet: any 3000 series, any 4000 series, the VIC20 and some of the 2000 series. All of these can be used, where suitable with any Commodore disc system to provide a file serving system and any other Commodore peripheral may be connected to Keynet through the master computer.

Keynet uses 12k bytes of RAM in the master unit, and no memory in slave units. All other operating software is in ROM on the Keynet printed circuit board. All stations may be run locally i.e. separately from the network, and with the exception of the master, can be turned on and off without affecting the network.

The Keynet printed circuit board is provided with switches to set variable parameters. These include selections of:

>Master or slave unit
>Device number (no. of units in network on master)
>Cable type (2, 3 or 4 twisted pairs)
>End or middle of line terminator
>ROM addresses
>Self-test

Keynet software

All the Keynet operating software is contained in ROM on the Keynet printed circuit board with the exception of some simple software which is used to open shared files. This is run from the master unit when the network is started up. Users' software can be interfaced to Keynet either through BASIC or machine code operation, and existing software only requires minor alterations to operate satisfactorily with Keynet.

Keynet provides security for network users' files by means of a password which must be given correctly before access to the file is permitted. There is also data record protection which prevents more than one station having access to a record at a time to update it. Once a station has read a record for the purposes of updating it, so other stations can have access for that purpose until the first station has completed its work.

The Amstrad Network

The Amstrad Network is supplied by Northern Computers of Frodsham, Cheshire, who are Amstrad's sole educational distributor in the UK. This fact gives some indication of where the main market for the Amstrad Network is seen, particularly as Amstrad Computers are now being recommended for educational use, sometimes in preference to Acorn's BBC model 'B'. Unlike Econet, the Amstrad Network is not restricted to the equipment supplied by the manufacturer but rather can be connected to nearly all available microcomputers and peripherals. The reason for this is found in the Amstrad Networks' background and development. It is in fact an extension of the Multilink network developed by Nine Tiles Ltd., discussed earlier in this chapter. It shares the same architecture and protocols as Multilink but differs in certain physical aspects and is being produced and distributed by Northern Computers as an entirely separate system. The physical differences between the two networks consist mainly of the 'ruggedising', or strengthening and foolproofing, necessary to make a system safe for use in educational establishments.

For these reasons, it is worthwhile treating the Amstrad Network as a separate system. Amstrad Computer's commanding position in the low-end computer market indicates that there will be a steady supply of users wishing to expand their facilities without the difficulties which may occur in going to other suppliers. The Amstrad Network is also likely to pick up customers from business and scientific organisations who only use small amounts of Amstrad equipment, but large amounts of business-oriented equipment such as Apple IIs, and IBM PCs. The fact that the Amstrad Network is compatible across the whole range of equipment, unlike Apple's and IBM's proprietary network offerings, could well make it the first choice for a network in these cases.

Amstrad Network hardware and software

The Amstrad Network has the following specification:

Topology	– ring
Access Method	– register or buffer insertion
Transmission	– baseband
Medium	– twisted pair cable
Range	– 1km between active nodes
Speed	– 250k baud
Max. no. of nodes	– 120 max.

and the following features:

1. A minimum of only two stations is needed to create the network.

2. By adding rings, an unlimited number of stations can be networked.

3. By adding filestore units, an unlimited amount of disc storage can be provided.

4. By adding more rings, an unlimited size of network can be created.

5. No central ring monitor station is needed.

6. Radio telecommunication links are available, allowing remote networks to be connected without expensive leased lines.

7. Virtually any mainframe, mini- and microcomputer, together with most peripherals, can be connected to the network, due to the availability of a wide variety of network interface units, including RS232C.

The network interfaces are based on ULA (Uncommitted Logic Array) technology, which allows a large number of functions to be squeezed into a small space. This means that the interfaces can be built into many of the computers on the network, reducing the amount of cabling required. The RS232C interfaces are stand-alone, self-powered versions and are used primarily to connect non-intelligent peripherals such as printers, plotters and terminals to the network.

Fig. 8.5 shows a typical Amstrad Network configuration, featuring the various types of interface unit.

A network station can be switched on or off, plugged in or out without affecting the network. If the ring is broken, intelligent stations are informed of the identity of the user nearest to the break. A fault in a computer on the network will not cause disruption unless it also causes the network socket box to fail.

Although the combination of 120 nodes maximum and a maximum active node spacing of 1km gives a maximum network size of 120km, to allow equipment to be switched off at random, the maximum recommended size of a single network is 3km. To increase this, the use of gateways to further networks is recommended.

The following interfaces and operating software are available:

1. Amstrad Network Interface. This unit connects to the expansion bus on the Amstrad computer and provides a second expansion bus to allow other

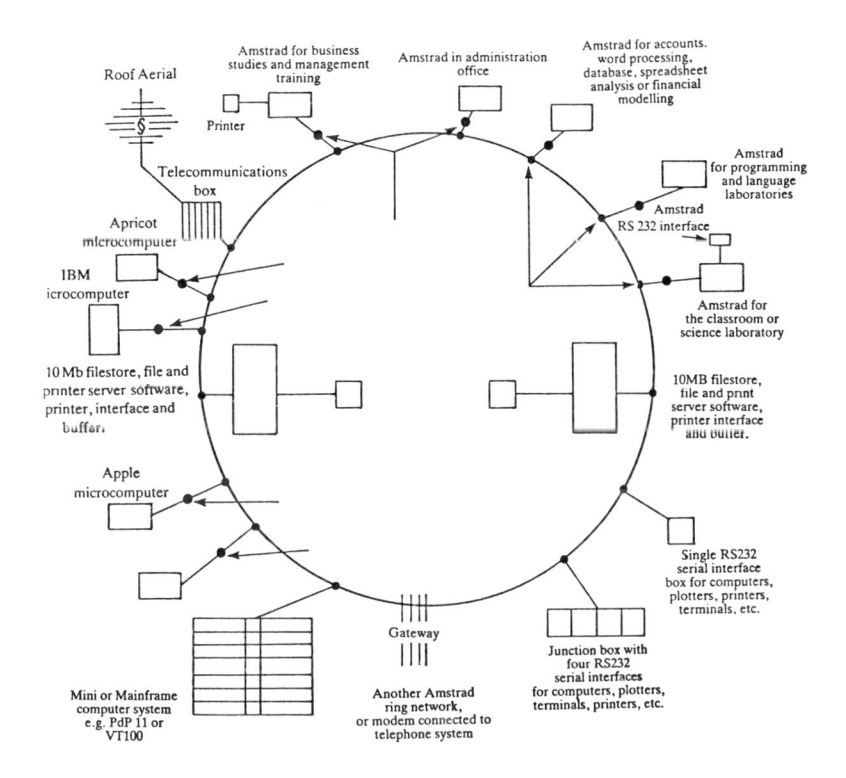

Fig. 8.5 The Amstrad Network

peripherals to be directly connected. The built-in software allows the computer access to network resources such as disc storage and printers, and also allows the unit to act as a terminal on the network and to communicate directly with programs running elsewhere in the network. Programs running under one operating system can access files stored in another computer, even when it runs a different operating system

2. Apple Network Interface. Plugs into the Apple II or IIe and allows access to standard Applesoft Basic files on the network. A network station driver software package is available to allow Apples running the CP/M operating system with a Z80 card to operate on the network.

3. Apricot Network Interface. Plugs into the expansion slot on the F, PC and Xi computers from Apricot. As well as network access, it provides other communications and clock/calendar facilities.

A network station driver software package is available to allow MSDOS and PCDOS operating systems to work with the network.

4. BBC Network Interface. Plugs into the disc controller socket on the BBC, and includes a Network File System (NFS) ROM. It provides networking and terminal emulation facilities.

The BBC computer can also be connected to the network through the Network Gateway if the RS232C version of the NFS ROM is used.

5. IBM PC Network Interface. Plugs into one of the expansion slots in the IBM PC, PC/XT, and PC/AT as well as IBM compatible systems. As well as network access, it provides communication and clock/calendar facilities.

Software facilities are available to allow MSDOS, PCDOS, CP/M 2 and CP/M+ operating systems to function with the network.

6. RS232C Interface boxes. With one or four RS232C connections to the network. Parameters such as baud rate, handshaking, and data format can all be simply adjusted to suit the user's applications. These units are used to connect computers and peripherals to the network.

7. Network Gateway. This is essentially a single RS232C box, but has extra software which allows it to transfer up to 63 different transmissions across the RS232C link simultaneously. It is, therefore, suitable for use as a gateway or bridge between two networks, with one unit on each network, directly connected through the RS232C link.

In addition, the network facilities can include:

1. The File Store. This is a hard-disc unit with a capacity of 10Mbytes, and includes printer interface along with buffering and print serving software. It can therefore provide all a network's file and print needs through a single network node. The file server can handle up to 40 separate connections to network nodes simultaneously.

2. The Telecommunications Box. This connects to a network gateway and is used to link two separate networks via radio transmission, which is particularly useful where the only other means of connection is through telephone or other leased lines.

The Amstrad Network intends to expand the range of interfaces and facilities available, which may well make it an attractive solution to commercial and technical network problems, as well as its current strength in educational areas.

CHAPTER 9
Future trends

This book is intended to give some idea of the development and present state of local area networks, and the way they impinge upon other aspects of modern communications technology. However, the nature of the field is one of constant change (and hopefully improvement) and even the time this book has been in preparation has seen major alterations, both in local area network technology and in the way it is perceived by users and potential users. It therefore seems appropriate to look at the way the technology will develop, and the way it will be used in the future. The following points all have some bearing on future trends in LANs.

Compatibility

The complete dominance achieved in recent years by IBM and its emulators in the personal computer market now makes it unwise for any manufacturer and supplier of local area networks to ignore this section of the market. LANs for IBM PCs and compatibles automatically have a large customer base. LANs not catering for these machines automatically lose access to this lucrative market. The same is, of course, true for all kinds of peripheral systems such as printers, memory backup systems, MODEMs and the like, and this circular process of peripheral supporting PC supporting peripheral has edged other hardware and software systems out of contention.

One-make LANs such as Acorn's Econet and Apple's Appletalk will be successful only insofar as their host computer systems will succeed and it is likely that more LAN manufacturers will produce PC-compatible interfaces, even those closely associated with competing microcomputer systems. Even the early leaders in the microcomputer field, such as Tandy and Commodore, are now producing machines with varying degrees of IBM compatibility.

Wide-range LANs, other than those supporting previously established communication standards like RS232C, will also base their product ranges around IBM PC-compatible interfaces. This preponderance of all things IBM will influence thinking in low-cost LAN development for the forseeable future and can be seen, in some ways, as the standardisation micro users have been clamouring for since the second microcomputer appeared. However, this standardisation by default leaves aside the thorny subject of standards for LANs rather than for the equipment they interconnect.

Standards and the high-cost, low-cost split

Local area networks are continuing on two development paths, which do not seem to be converging. These two paths can be described as the high-cost, high-performance path, and the low-cost, low-performance path, bearing in mind that cost and performance in this context are purely relative terms.

The high-cost, high performance development, typified by Ethernet and its myriad supporters, implies strong adherence to whatever national (USA) and international standards are applicable, ensuring that different manufacturers and suppliers can provide compatible components and complete systems. In general the standards involved are mostly the IEEE 802 committee's and the International Standards Organisation's OSI model (see section on standards). Both these standards are well-established and well supported, and to a large extent compatible.

This kind of standardisation is very attractive to large business users who view continuity and second sources of supply as more important than low cost. The relatively high performance of these types of LANs is also essential as the standards were originally produced with large scale business and research organisations in mind. There is no doubt that these standards and networks will flourish and provide the technological lead in the LAN field, as data rates increase and the number of potential users expands rapidly.

Meanwhile a new class of users has appeared, brought into the LAN market by the proliferation of low-cost computing power and the need to connect it all together in order to use it efficiently. Schools, small businesses and research organisations all come into this category. The common denominator in this class is perennial lack of funds, making high-performance, high-cost networks impractical as a solution to their communication problems. These users are more inclined to choose a solution in which standardisation and compatibility come a very poor second to cheapness. Most of this group of users will be willing to sacrifice operating speed if it saves them money and are more inclined to either work with limited facilities or devote time and effort to circumventing problems inherent in the design of low-performance, low-cost networks. Bottom-end users are a growing group, both in real terms and, more rapidly, as a proportion of LAN users. So far, they have not exerted any substantial effect on general LAN development as they are not the customer base towards which research and development is directed, but it is likely that the market they represent will not be ignored by the main LAN developers for long.

This may give rise to a new standard for low-cost, low-performance LANs, conforming perhaps to the OSI 7-layer model but fundamentally different from the high-power LANs currently leading the standardisation drive.

The British Microcomputer Manufacturers Group (BMMG) are currently proposing a standard which may go some way towards this but as the BMMG consists mostly of small manufacturers, and their proposals do not yet have any international acceptance it remains to be seen whether their efforts will bear fruit. It is important that manufacturers do cooperate to produce agreed standards, but it is equally important that the agreement is international and that its backers have sufficient influence to promote it.

One new proposal that will undoubtedly find favour is the Manufacturing Automation Protocol (MAP) developed for General Motors. MAP has been around for some time but has been restricted to the automated manufacturing environment where networking is still in its infancy. However, the recent announcement that an office automation subset called Technical and Office Protocols (TOP) has been developed has been greeted with enthusiasm by manufacturing and computing giants alike. On the industrial side, General Motors are backed by international organisations like Boeing, Volkswagen and British Aerospace, whilst computer manufacturers including IBM have agreed to support MAP.

MAP is also said to conform to the International Standards Organisation OSI seven-layer model, making it compatible with most other high performance networks. This widespread support and compatibility, together with the tremendous potential for networking in industrial and manufacturing applications, could mean that MAP may emerge as the one network standard on which everyone can agree in the future.

Falling costs and chip sets

One of the accepted pieces of wisdom about local area networks is that as more of the network functions are integrated on a chip the cost of the network will fall. But will it? It is true that one integrated circuit will cost less than five of the same circuit, but whereas the integrated circuits currently used in most LANs are mass-market devices produced in thousands if not millions, and sold at competitive rates, chips specifically designed for networking have a much narrower market, which must mean that costs per chip will remain relatively high until every intelligent digital electronic device has a network node installed as standard during manufacture. However, there are other advantages to be gained by using specially-designed networking integrated circuits, particularly where size and power consumption are critical factors. Using custom integrated circuits allows networking to be built into the coming generation of portable, battery-powered systems, as well as allowing more space for other things in desktop computers and peripherals.

Manufacturers are now offering networking chip sets: Intel has an Ethernet set, and Texas Instruments have announced a set for use with the much-heralded IBM Token Ring LAN, and there is no doubt that these integrated circuits will be generally used to produce a new generation of networking equipment, but LANs lend themselves very well to another branch of integrated circuit technology, the Uncomitted Logic Array (ULA). These devices can be produced to perform a particular function in relatively small numbers, without incurring any of the cost penalties usually associated with small-batch manufacture of semiconductor devices. This has made them popular with smaller LAN manufacturers and both the Multilink and Amstrad LANs featured in Chapter 8 incorporate ULAs.

ULAs and specially-designed chip sets will contribute to a reduction in the cost of high-powered, high-cost LANs, but the cost reduction per node often mentioned by manufacturers and analysts may be misleading. Node costs are not the only cost in a network. In fact, cabling cost may well exceed the other hardware costs in some situations, and no amount of custom integrated circuits is going to shorten the cable. High-performance baseband LANs, such as Ethernet need high-quality cable and whilst the economies of scale apply to cable just as they do to semiconductors, the LAN market's relative smallness, and the intrinsic expense of the material in the cable may combine to thwart the sought-after price reductions. Cabling and installation costs for this type of network are likely to remain relatively high in the forseeable future.

In contrast, costs for broadband LANs are concentrated in the node, which must include a modem. Cables and connectors used are produced in huge quantities for the cable TV market and are, therefore, relatively cheap already. Hopes for drastic cost reductions in broadband LANs centre on the increasing demand for modems and the possibilities of integrating modem functions onto chips. There is speculation that broadband systems may become as cheap as equivalent baseband networks if this happens. Broadband LANs would then be a very attractive alternative, considering their inherent versatility.

Low-cost, low-performance baseband LANs will continue to exist, using cheap components and cheap cabling or in some cases, no cabling at all. One British LAN, Nectarring, transmits its signals through the cables providing AC power to the network, thus eliminating the need for any additional cabling costs. This sort of cost-conscious approach is bound to find favour with users.

The high cost of high-performance baseband systems has been recognised by some manufacturers as a problem and a reduced form of Ethernet, popularly known as 'Cheapernet', is now available. It is however, still a much more powerful and expensive system than many of the low-cost baseband networks.

Network-to-network connections

Once equipment is connected together using a LAN, users invariably find that the whole system would benefit from connections to another system. The logical step is to install some kind of network-to-network connection, either to allow two systems to share facilities, or to allow a small, low-performance LAN to act as a feeder to a bigger network. This larger network might be a high-performance LAN, a WAN using radio and telecom links, or a distributed mainframe computing system. The term 'bridge' is normally used for a connection between two similar networks, whereas 'gateway' is normally used to describe a link between two dissimilar networks.

It is obvious that bridges and gateways will proliferate in the near future as users seek to make the best use of the available resources, and these inter-network products are likely to become almost as common as the networks they support. Already, manufacturers are producing equipment to link LANs to public networks such as the X25 Packet-Switched network, an indication that the future of low-cost LANs may lie as much in acting as front ends for larger systems as in stand-alone operation. In future, the usefulness of a local area network will be judged, among other things, on the number of other systems it can be connected to.

General

As a general rule, local area networks of all types are going to become more common, and at the same time, more invisible. Microcomputer manufacturers will eventually come to some sort of agreement about networking and start to include LAN facilities within their equipment as standard, in the way Apple are currently doing with the Macintosh and LaserWriter. This facility has been largely ignored in the general speculation about the Macintosh, but it represents a significant step forward in terms of integrating LANs with the systems they are meant to serve. When other manufacturers adopt this approach LAN software will be contained within the normal operating software of the computer, and networks will be designed as single entities rather than as a group of individual units with various interconnections. The LAN will cease to be an afterthought and become the starting point from which all systems are planned.

However, the integrated approach to local area networking requires both manufacturer and customer to see things the same way, and it may take some time before the general level of awareness of the subject is such that integrated systems from single or multiple sources become a common occurrence. In the meantime, users must continue to pick and choose the network that best suits their particular needs from within whatever budget constraints exist, and struggle against the difficulties imposed by all manner of incompatible and inadequate hardware and software.

Appendix A:
Available LANs

This section of the book is designed to give the potential user information about the Local Area Networks currently available in the UK. The nature of the technology means that some new suppliers will not be included, some older suppliers will have gone out of business or changed their product ranges, and nearly all of the active suppliers will have improved and expanded their product ranges. Most of the products featured are complete LAN systems but a separate section has been added to provide information on a representative sample of Ethernet component suppliers.

Although the emphasis of this book is on low-cost Local Area Networks, LANs in all price ranges are included in this section. This is done to give the fullest information possible about available LANs. Similarly, no price information is included, other than the designation "low-cost", as these vary with time and more drastically with the applications for which the LAN is used. For up-to-date price information, contact the relevant supplier.

Entries in this appendix are listed by network name, in alphabetical order, except where there is no fixed product name. In these cases, the entry is under the manufacturer's name.

Advance Net

Supplier: Hewlett-Packard UK

Technology:
Topology	bus
Access	CSMA/CD
Transmission	baseband
Medium	coaxial cable
Range	500m
Speed	$10\,Mbs^{-1}$
No. of nodes	N/A

Compatible equipment: Hewlett-Packard 9000 series Computers

Comments: AdvanceNet has been produced by Hewlett-Packard for their own computer systems and is probably not of interest to anyone who is not operating or communicating with HP equipment. HP are committed to the IEEE 802.3 standard for LANs and users are offered an upgrade path from the earlier Ethernet-based systems to the slightly different IEEE 802.3 equipment now on offer. AdvanceNet includes both the hardware interfaces and the operating software required to control the network.

Amstrad Network

Supplier: Northern Computers Ltd

Technology:
Topology	ring
Access	register insertion
Transmission	baseband
Medium	twisted-pair cable
Range	1km between nodes
Speed	250kbs^{-1}
No. of nodes	120

Compatible equipment: Amstrad Computers, IBM PC and compatibles, Apple II, Apricot Computers, BBC computer, Amstrad Filestores, RS232 devices.

Comments: The Amstrad Network is a low-cost, general purpose LAN designed originally for the Amstrad computers. It is now compatible with most popular microcomputers and seems set for a long and successful future. The network includes cabling, hardware interfaces, operating software, file server units, and gateways to other networks, including radio links.

AppleTalk

Supplier: Apple UK

Technology:
Topology	bus
Access	CSMA/CD
Transmission	baseband
Medium	shielded twisted-pair
Range	300m
Speed	230.4 Kbs^{-1}
No. of nodes	32

Compatible equipment: Apple Macintosh, Laserwriter, interface development under way for other Apple products, file and disc servers, and IBM PC's.

Comments: AppleTalk is Apple's proprietary network for the upper end of their product range, and currently only of interest to Macintosh users and prospective users, although this may change when other interfaces are developed. Interestingly, all the necessary network hardware and software is contained within the standard Macintosh and the AppleTalk kit consists of little more than cables and connectors. Apple claim that despite the relatively low data rate, true data transfer is as fast as other systems with higher rates, due to the efficiency of the embedded hardware and software.

Apricot Networks

Supplier: Apricot UK

Technology:
Topology	bus
Access	CSMA/CD
Transmission	baseband
Medium	twisted pair
Range	2000 ft.
Speed	1 Mbs^{-1}
No. of nodes	32

Compatible equipment: Apricot F1, F1e, F2, F10, FP, PC, Xi 10, Xi 20, 32/10 File server, 32/20 File server, 32/80 File server Apricot Bank tape cartridge unit.

Comments: Apricot Networks are Apricot's proprietary LAN systems, based around the three hard-disc file-server units which are essentially Apricot computers minus keyboard and display. The LAN technology is the ubiquitous Omninet from Corvus (q.v.). An obvious choice of system for multiple-Apricot users. Both hardware and software is included in the network.

ARCnet

Supplier: Datapoint UK

Technology:
Topology	bus
Access	token-passing
Transmission	baseband
Medium	coaxial cable
Range	4 miles

Speed   2.5 Mbs.$^{-1}$
No. of nodes   255

Compatible equipment: IBM PC and compatible systems, IBM PC AT, Datapoint computers, Convergent Technology equipment.

Comments: ARCnet was conceived as a network for Datapoint's own computing equipment but has proved popular for other equipment as well. It is now well established, particularly in the US and can be connected to other systems such as PABXs and line-of-sight transmitters, to provide extended networks.

ASTNET

Supplier: AST Europe

Technology:
Topology	bus
Access	CSMA/CD
Transmission	baseband
Medium	coaxial cable
Range	1km.
Speed	800 kbs^{-1}
No. of nodes	180

Compatible equipment: IBM PC and compatibles.

Comments: A third-party network desgined primarily for the huge IBM PC market. Gateways to other systems are available.

BabyNet

Supplier: Interlekt Electronics

Technology:
Topology	full duplex multidrop
Access	adaptive polling
Transmission	baseband
Medium	N/A
Range	N/A
Speed	N/A
No. of nodes	22 at master + 64 system nodes

Compatible equipment: Any RS232 device.

Comments: Babynet is a development of intelligent terminal switch technology and would normally be used to connect a large number of mainframe computer ports. However, its versatility makes it of interest to LAN users.

Cable Stream

Supplier: Information Technology Ltd (ITL)

Technology:
Topology	bus
Access	CSMA/CD
Transmission	broadband
Medium	coaxial cable
Range	50 km
Speed	15.4 Mbs^{-1}
No. of nodes	64000

Compatible equipment: Wide range of microcomputer, minicomputers, mainframes, modems and other equipment.

Comments: Cable Stream is the generic term used by ITL for a wide range of networking services including hardware and software. The LAN aspect of Cable Stream uses the LocalNet LAN from Sytek (q.v.) which is also available in its own right.

Cachenet

Supplier: Eicon

Technology:
Topology	bus/tree(SASI/SCASI)
Access	CSMA/CD
Transmission	baseband
Medium	ribbon cable
Range	100m
Speed	11 Mbs^{-1}
No. of nodes	21

Compatible equipment: IBM PC and AT, Apple II, NEC APC

Comments: Cachenet is primarily designed as a file server system for small groups of PCs and includes a file server unit as standard. The

'Cache' part of its name comes from the inclusion of a 256k byte cache memory which holds information which is frequently called from disc, thus reducing disc access time and increasing the overall network speed. A serial bus system with extended range will soon be available.

Casenet

Supplier: Computer and Systems Engineering (CASE)

Technology:
	Topology	bus
	Access	CSMA/CD
	Transmission	base– and broadband
	Medium	coaxial cable
	Range	500m
	Speed	10 Mbs^{-1}
	No. of nodes	1024

Compatible equipment: CASE telecoms equipment, RS232C equipment, most types of computer.

Comments: Casenet is CASE's version of Ungermann-Bass's Net/One (q.v.), one of the most popular US networks, with enhancements allowing it to work with CASE telecoms equipment.

Chain

Supplier: Research Machines Ltd (RML)

Technology:
	Topology	bus
	Access	CSMA/CD
	Transmission	baseband
	Medium	coaxial cable
	Range	1.2km
	Speed	800 kbs.$^{-1}$
	No. of nodes	16

Compatible equipment: RML Network Server, RML 480Z workstation.

Comments: Chain is designed specifically for RMLs own equipment, which is sold heavily to educational markets. The first choice for multiple RML users, otherwise not of great interest. Based on the Zilog Z-Net (q.v.).

CLAN

Supplier: CASU

Technology:

Topology	bus
Access	token-passing
Transmission	baseband
Medium	coaxial cable
Range	4 miles
Speed	2.5 Mbs^{-1}
No. of nodes	255

Compatible equipment: Casu PC, Arcnet-based equipment.

Comments: CLAN is a version of ARCnet (q.v.) supplied by Casu for their own PCs.

Clearway

Supplier: Real Time Developments

Technology:

Topology	ring
Access	register insertion
Transmission	baseband
Medium	coaxial cable
Range	500m between nodes
Speed	56 kbs^{-1}
No. of nodes	99

Compatible equipment: Any RS232C device.

Comments: Clearway is a simple, low-cost network aimed at users with a small number of microcomputers and peripherals. Cost-effective and highly recommended.

Cluster/One

Supplier: Zynar

Technology:
Topology	bus
Access	CSMA/CD
Transmission	baseband
Medium	multi-core cable
Range	300m.
Speed	240 kbs^{-1}
No. of nodes	256

Compatible equipment: Apple II, Apple III

Comments: Cluster/One from the American Nestar company is one of the earliest low-cost networks, and is very suitable for users with a number of Apples in a small area. Its continued success depends on the future of the Apple II family of microcomputers.

C-Net

Supplier: Control-C

Technology:
Topology	bus
Access	token passing
Transmission	baseband
Medium	coaxial cable
Range	N/A
Speed	500Kbs^{-1}
No. of nodes	64

Compatible equipment: ICL PC, IBM PC, Apricot computers.

Comments: Designed for use with Digital Research's DR-Net software and Concurrent-DOS. It is mainly used with ICL equipment.

Codex 4000

Supplier: Motorola Information Systems

Technology:
Topology	bus
Access	CSMA/CD
Transmission	baseband/broadband
Medium	coaxial cable
Range	500m baseband, 15,240m broadband
Speed	10Mbs^{-1}
No. of nodes	1024 baseband

Compatible equipment: RS232C equipment, IEEE-488 bus equipment, DEC DR-11-W/B equipment, IBM PC, XT, compatibles.

Comments: Codex 4000 is a range of LAN interface equipment with outputs to both Ethernet-compatible baseband cables and CATV-compatible broadband cables within each device. A very versatile system.

Domain

Supplier: Apollo Computer UK

Technology:
Topology	bus
Access	token passing
Transmission	baseband
Medium	coaxial cable
Range	1km between nodes
Speed	12Mbs^{-1}
No. of nodes	>1000

Compatible equipment: Apollo computers and workstations, RS232C devices, Multibus devices, IBM equipment, Telecom equipment.

Comments: Domain is an integral part of the Apollo computers and workstations and is meant primarily as a very high speed network for them. Mainly of interest to those who need the graphics and number-crunching power of Apollo products.

Econet

Supplier: Acorn Computers

Technology:
Topology	bus
Access	CSMA/CD
Transmission	baseband
Medium	twisted pair cable
Range	1km
Speed	307Kbs^{-1}
No. of nodes	254

Compatible equipment: BBC computer, Acorn computers.

Comments: Econet is Acorn's own LAN for their own product, particularly the BBC microcomputer. Its low cost makes it particularly attractive to educational users who purchase BBC computers in large amounts.

EasyLan

Supplier Tashkl Computer Systems

Technology:
Topology	star
Access	polling
Transmission	baseband
Medium	coaxial cable
Range	300 ft.
Speed	19.2Kbs^{-1}
No. of nodes	10

Compatible equipment: IBM PC and compatibles.

Comments: A very low-cost system consisting initially of connecting cable and software as the network uses the PC printer port. Expansion of the network requires the installation of further printer ports in the central unit.

Elan

Supplier: GEAC Computers Ltd

Technology:
	Topology	bus
	Access	CSMA/CD
	Transmission	baseband
	Medium	coaxial cable
	Range	500m
	Speed	10Mbs^{-1}
	No. of nodes	1024

Compatible equipment: GEAC equipment

Comments: Elan is an integrated part of GEAC's networking product and service range, and is based on Ungermann-Bass's Net/One LAN.

G-Net

Supplier: Persona

Technology:
	Topology	bus
	Access	CSMA/CD
	Transmission	N/A
	Medium	coaxial cable
	Range	N/A
	Speed	1.43Mbs^{-1}
	No. of nodes	255

Compatible equipment: IBM PC and compatibles

Grapevine

Supplier: CASE Communications Ltd

Technology:
	Topology	star
	Access	N/A

Transmission	broadband
Medium	twisted pair cable
Range	3km
Speed	9.6Kbs^{-1}
No. of nodes	N/A

Compatible equipment: RS232C equipment.

Comments: Grapevine consists of access units attached to extensions on a PABX, and a CASE distribution unit in parallel with the PABX switchboard. Grapevine thus uses the previously-installed telephone wires and must be of interest to anyone wishing to install a LAN where there is already a PABX.

Hi-Net

Supplier: Digital Microsystems Inc. (DMI)

Technology:
Topology	bus
Access	multidrop (polling)
Transmission	baseband
Medium	twisted pair cable
Range	4000ft
Speed	500Kbs^{-1}
No. of nodes	32

Compatible equipment: DMI microcomputers, IBM PC, Apricot, Mainframes.

Comments: Hi-Net is a complete system based on DMI's own proprietary microcomputers and file servers, although PC interfaces are suitable. Not a general purpose LAN.

Hydra

Supplier: Dataview Ltd

Technology:
Topology	bus
Access	CSMA/CD
Transmission	baseband
Medium	4-wire cable
Range	250Kbs^{-1}

Speed   1km
No. of nodes   128

Compatible equipment: All Commodore (CBM) equipment.

Comments: Hydra, along with Commodore's own Keynet (q.v.), is one of the few LANs designed specially for CBM equipment. Its low cost and specialisation must make it an obvious choice for multiple CBM users.

Hyperbus

Supplier: Network Systems Corporation (NSC)

Technology: Topology   bus
                  Access   CSMA/CD
                  Transmission   baseband
                  Medium   coaxial cable
                  Range   N/A
                  Speed $6.312 Mbs^{-1}$
                  No. of nodes   N/A

Compatible equipment: RS232C equipment, IBM 3270 equipment 16 bit-parallel interfaces.

Comments: Hyperbus is part of a combined network system developed by NSC which includes Hyperchannel, a very high speed network for mini- and mainframe computer communications. Generally directed at the high-performance market.

IBM PC Network

Supplier: IBM UK

Technology: Topology   tree
                  Access   CSMA/CD
                  Transmission   broadband
                  Medium   coaxial cable
                  Range   609.6m
                  Speed $2 Mbs^{-1}$
                  No. of nodes   72

Compatible equipment: IBM PC, XT, and AT, and compatibles.

Comments: IBM's own network for their ubiquitous PC. There are many third party LAN suppliers who will offer IBM tough competition both on price and features in the market. Operating software is included.

IBM PC Cluster

Supplier: IBM UK

Technology:
Topology	bus
Access	CSMA/CD
Transmission	baseband
Medium	coaxial cable
Range	1km
Speed	375Kbs^{-1}
No. of nodes	64

Compatible equipment: IBM PC, XT, and compatibles.

Comments: A lower price, simpler LAN from IBM, in comparison with their PC Network, but likely to fulfil the needs of most users. Operating software is included.

IBM Token Ring Network

Supplier: IBM

Technology:
Topology	ring
Access	token passing
Transmission	baseband
Medium	shielded twisted pair
Range	N/A
Speed	4Mbs^{-1}
No. of nodes	260

Compatible equipment: IBM PC, portable PC, XT and AT.

Comments: IBM's much-heralded network, finally unveiled in late 1985. As with all IBM systems, the complete range of hardware and software, including cabling, is available. IBM 3270 Terminal Emulation and connections to IBM's PC Network (q.v.) are available. IBM have published all the network specifications and are encouraging other manufacturers to supply system components. Texas Instruments are producing the specialised integrated circuits for general sale. It seems likely, given IBM's pre-eminent position, that there will shortly be as much equipment and software available for the IBM Token Ring as there is presently for Ethernet. The Token Ring conforms to IEEE 802.5 and ECMA 89 standards making it widely acceptable to European and American users, and its future seems assured.

Infaplug

Supplier: Infa Communications

Technology:
	Topology	ring
	Access	register instertion
	Transmission	baseband
	Medium	twisted pair cable
	Range	800m between active nodes
	Speed	115Kbs^{-1}
	No. of nodes	255

Compatible equipment: RS232C devices

Comments: Infaplug is a low cost network designed for use with a variety of microcomputers and peripherals, hence the universal RS232C interface. Interestingly, the nodes are powered from the ring cable rather than the user's equipment or the mains. A cost-effective solution for anyone looking for low cost networking without frills. Operating software is also available for PCs.

Instanet

Supplier: Micom-Borer Ltd

Technology:
	Topology	bus
	Access	CSMA/CD
	Transmission	baseband
	Medium	coaxial cable
	Range	500m
	Speed	10Mbs^{-1}
	No. of nodes	1024

Compatible equipment: RS232C devices, IBM PC and compatibles, DEC Qbus and Unibus equipment, Intel Multibus equipment.

Comments: Instanet is an Ethernet-based LAN with emphasis on networking terminals to minicomputers. Software is available to run under VMS and UNIX operating systems on minis, and a Network File Server package is available for the IBM PC. Micom-Borer also provide a Data PABX network.

Interlekt ITS

Supplier: Interlekt Electronics

Technology:
	Topology	star
	Access	N/A
	Transmission	baseband
	Medium	RS232C standard
	Range	RS232C standard
	Speed	9600bs^{-1}
	No. of nodes	16

Compatible equipment: RS232C devices.

Comments: The Interlekt Intelligent (Asynchronous) Terminal Switch is in effect a 16-arm star network for connecting mini and microcomputers and peripherals, as well as connecting terminals to mainframes.

Isolan

Supplier: BICC Data Networks Ltd

Technology:
	Topology	bus
	Access	CSMA/CD
	Transmission	baseband
	Medium	coaxial cable
	Range	500m
	Speed	10Mbs^{-1}
	No. of nodes	1024

Compatible equipment: RS232C equipment, IBM PC and compatibles.

Comments: Isolan is a system of network components designed to conform to all the major standards for 10Mb CSMA/CD LANs ie. IEEE 802.3, software is also available and the Isolan Fan-Out unit, designed to interface 8 RS232C devices to the bus can also be operated in stand-alone node as an 8-node star network.

Keynet

Supplier: Commodore UK

Technology:
Topology	bus/tree
Access	master/slave pseudo-poll
Transmission	baseband
Medium	4 twisted pair cable
Range	>1km
Speed	250 Kbs^{-1}
No. of nodes	250

Compatible equipment: Nearly all Commodore computers.

Comments: Keynet is Commodore's own LAN system for their range of computers and includes networking software. Commodore machines are neglected by LAN manufacturers and Keynet, with the exception of Hydra (q.v.), is the only network available. A low cost system.

LAN/1

Supplier: Interactive Systems, 3M UK

Technology:
Topology	bus
Access	token passing
Transmission	broadband
Medium	coaxial cable
Range	7 miles
Speed	2.5Mbs^{-1}
No. of nodes	2000 per channel
	5 channels

Compatible equipment: RS232C devices.

Comments: LAN/1 is a comprehensive set of networking equipment available from 3M. As the specification shows, it is a high-performance LAN designed to be used over wide areas with a large number of nodes. 3M also provide a design and maintenance service.

Lincmaster

Supplier: Master Systems Ltd

Technology:
	Topology	star
	Access	N/A
	Transmission	broadband
	Medium	twisted pair
	Range	N/A
	Speed	19.2Kbs^{-1}
	No. of nodes	unlimited

Compatible equipment: RS232C equipment.

Comments: Lincmaster uses an installed PABX system as the transmission medium, filtering out data from voice at the PABX switch and routing it separately.. Telephone and RS232C device both plug into a single Lincmaster box which then connects to the Telecom wall socket. Of interest to users with a PABX and a large number of low-speed data users.

Localnet

Supplier: Network Technology Ltd

Technology:
	Topology	bus
	Access	CSMA/CD
	Transmission	broadband
	Medium	coaxial cable
	Range	50km
	Speed	15.4Mbs^{-1}
	No. of nodes	64000

Compatible equipment: RS232C equipment.

Comments: Localnet is a well-established broadband LAN and is popular in the US. It is sold by other manufacturers under other names as part of their own network systems. Localnet is suitable for large networks, especially where voice traffic is to be included.

LSI Net

Supplier: LSI Computers

Technology:
	Topology	tree
	Access	token-passing
	Transmission	N/A
	Medium	coaxial cable
	Range	N/A
	Speed	2.5Mbs.$^{-1}$
	No. of nodes	255

Compatible equipment: LSI Octopus range of computers.

Comments: a network currently of restricted interest.

M24 R

Supplier: Raindrop Computers

Technology:
	Topology	bus
	Access	N/A
	Transmission	baseband
	Medium	twisted pair cable
	Range	4000ft
	Speed	1Mbs^{-1}
	No. of nodes	unlimited

Compatible equipment: Olivetti M24, IBM PC compatibles.

Comments: M24R is based around a modified Olivetti M24 computer which acts as a file server for the network. It is a good value-for-money system but needs the BOS operating system to function.

Microlan

Supplier: ICL

Technology:
	Topology	bus
	Access	CSMA/CD
	Transmission	baseband
	Medium	coaxial cable

Range	N/A
Speed	1Mbs.$^{-1}$
No. of nodes	16

Compatible equipment: ICL DRS 20 Microcomputer and associated peripherals.

Comments: Microlan is ICL's LAN specially for the DRS microcomputers. ICL's network strategy also embraces more general-purpose networks such as Macrolan, for linking mainframe computers, and OSlan (q.v.) which conforms to international standards.

Micro Prod/Net

Supplier: CCA

Technology:	Topology	bus/tree
	Access	token passing
	Transmission	baseband
	Medium	coaxial cable
	Range	4 miles
	Speed	2.5Mbs^{-1}
	No. of nodes	255

Compatible equipment: IBM PC, AT and compatibles.

Comments: Micro Prod/Net hardware is based on Arcnet (q.v.) and the operating software is the Port multitasking OS. It has a variety of gateways to host systems and is designed to run with Host Prod/Net which runs on IBM mainframes.

Minstrel

Supplier: HM Systems

Technology:	Topology	bus
	Access	token-passing
	Transmission	baseband
	Medium	coaxial cable
	Range	4 miles
	Speed	2.5Mbs^{-1}
	No. of nodes	255

Compatible equipment: IBM PC and compatibles, Apricot, S100 bus systems.

Comments: Minstrel is a combination of LAN and multi-user computer systems. The heart of the system is the Minstrel 2 box containing a file server running the Turbo DOS operating system. The expansion sockets in the box can contain either shared processors for multi-user computing or network interfaces for LAN use. The hardware for the LAN is based on Arcnet (q.v.) and there is a large range of peripherals available, including modems and telex facilities. A versatile and interesting system that covers most requirements.

Multilink

Supplier: Nine Tile Computer Systems, Hawker Siddeley Dynamics Engineering.

Technology:	Topology	ring
	Access	register insertions
	Transmission	baseband
	Medium	twisted pair cable
	Range	1km between active nodes
	Speed	$250 Kbs^{-1}$
	No. of nodes	125

Compatible equipment: IBM PC and compatibles, Apricot, Apple IIe, Amstrad, BBC, DEC Unibus equipment, Olivetti, DEC LSI-11 bus equipment, Intel Multibus equipment, S-100 bus equipment, Epson QX10, QX16, RS232C equipment.

Comments: Multilink is a versatile, low cost LAN of interest to anyone with a wide variety of equipment to interconnect. Simple Net operating software is also available for the microcomputer interfaces. See Chapter 8 for more detail.

Net/One

Supplier: Ungermann-Bass Ltd

Technology:	Topology	bus, tree
	Access	CSMA

Transmission	baseband, broadband
Medium	coaxial cable
Range	500m, 10km
Speed	10Mbs^{-1}, 5Mbs^{-1}
No. of nodes	1024, 250
	baseband network

Compatible equipment: IBM PC, RS232C devices.

Comments: Together with Datapoint's Arcnet (q.v.) Net/One has become the basis of a variety of different LAN packages from various manufacturers. It is a high-performance network in both baseband and broadband forms, the former being Ethernet-compatible. The baseband Net/One has been long-established in the US and is likely to be one of the more popular high performance systems in the UK.

Net/Plus

Supplier: Data Translation

Technology:
Topology	bus
Access	CSMA/CD
Transmission	baseband
Medium	coaxial cable
Range	500m
Speed	10Mbs^{-1}
No. of nodes	1024

Compatible equipment: DEC minicomputers, Data General minicomputers Intel Multibus systems, RS232C devices.

Comments: Net/Plus is the name for Interlan's family of Ethernet products. Networking software is available for most popular PCs, driving the RS232C connections. Available as a complete system or as components.

Nectar Ring

Supplier: Nectar

Technology:
Topology	bus
Access	N/A

Transmission Medium	broadband mains power cables
Range	4800bs^{-1}
Speed	N/A
No. of nodes	N/A

Compatible equipment: RS232C equipment.

Comments: NectarRing is unusual in that it uses a building's installed mains wiring to transmit data, by modulating a h.f. carrier with the data signal. This is the principal used in cordless intercoms and similar devices and has the advantage of doing away with separate wiring for the network. A low cost system.

Nimbus

Supplier: Research Machines Ltd

Technology:		
	Topology	bus
	Access	CSMA/CD
	Transmission	baseband
	Medium	coaxial cable
	Range	1200m
	Speed	0.8Mbs^{-1}
	No. of nodes	64

Compatible equipment: Research Machines Nimbus series microcomputers.

Comments: The Nimbus network is designed specially for use with RML's Nimbus computers, which run a networking version of the MS-DOS operating system. Of interest to users wishing to install a complete MS-DOS-based network.

NetWare

Supplier: Novell Data Systems.

Technology: Various

Compatible equipment: IBM PC, XT, AT and compatibles, Motorola 68000-based systems.

Comments: Novell provide NetWare Operating System software on its own, for previously installed LAN's, and as a part of a complete LAN package based on various hardware proprietary LANs. The packages available are based on Arcnet (q.v.), Omninet (q.v.), a star LAN centred on a Motorola 6800-based file server called NetWare/S, and a CSMA/CD bus network based on Z80 plug-in interfaces for IBM PC, called NetWare/G, among others. Netware itself is available for most popular LAN's including the IBM PC Net, Ethernet and Plan 2000. A large range of functions are included within NetWare.

Omninet

Supplier: Keen Computers, Vistec.

Technology:
	Topology	bus
	Access	CSMA.CD
	Transmission	baseband
	Medium	twisted pair cable
	Range	1.2km
	Speed	1Mbs^{-1}
	No. of nodes	64

Compatible equipment: Corvus Concept, IBM PC and compatibles, DEC Rainbow, Apple equipment, Texas Professional.

Comments: Omninet was developed by Corvus Systems for use with microcomputers including their own Concept range. It has proved very popular as a system on which to base LAN packages and is resold by a number of third-party suppliers such as Novell (q.v.). A subset of Omninet, called Omnishare, is also available.

Orbis

Supplier: Orbis/Acorn Computers

Technology:
	Topology	ring
	Access	empty slot
	Transmission	baseband
	Medium	twisted pair cable
	Range	300m between nodes
	Speed	10/20Mbs^{-1}
	No. of nodes	256

Compatible equipment: DEC PDP and LS1-11, DG Nova CA LS1-4, Acorn System 3.

Comments: The Orbis LAN is essentially a Cambridge Ring available in two speed versions. Its interfaces are mostly for minicomputers but Econet (q.v.) compatibility is provided through the Acorn system.

OpenNET

Supplier: Intel

Technology: Ethernet

Compatible equipment: Intel Multibus systems, IBM PC and compatibles.

Comments: OpenNET is Intels' implementation of Ethernet. The combination of hardware, software and XENIX operating system is designed to link groups of IBM PC's to Multibus systems acting as file servers through an Ethernet link – essentially a specialised Ethernet package.

OSNET

Supplier: ICL

Technology:

	Topology	bus
	Access	CSMA/CD
	Transmission	baseband
	Medium	coaxial cable
	Range	500m
	Speed	10Mbs^{-1}
	No. of nodes	1024

Compatible equipment: RS232C devices.

Comments: OSNET is ICL's OSI-compatible network system and includes hardware and software, the software residing in a network management station. The bus itself – OSLAN – is fully compatible with IEEE 802.3 standard and is, in effect, Ethernet. The network management software provides a wide range of services on top of what would otherwise be a simple Ethernet LAN, including various connection options and protocol conversions.

PCNet

Supplier: Ferrarri

Technology:
Topology	bus
Access	CSMA/CD
Transmission	baseband
Medium	coaxial cable
Range	N/A
Speed	$1Mbs^{-1}$
No. of nodes	255

Compatible equipment: IBM PC and compatibles.

Comments:

PC2PC/Decision Net

Supplier: NCR

Technology:
Topology	bus
Access	CSMA/CD
Transmission	baseband
Medium	coaxial cable
Range	1000ft
Speed	$1Mbs^{-1}$
No. of nodes	64

Compatible equipment: IBM PCs and compatibles, NCR Decision Mate, Apple equipment.

Comments: PC2PC and NCR's Decision Net are based on the same technology, with Decision Net offering interfaces for Apple products as well as NCR and IBM equipment. File serving on Decision Net must be via a Modus or microModus file server, whereas PC2PC can use any IBM machine.

PC Path

Supplier: Logitek

Technology:
Topology	bus
Access	CSMA/CD

Transmission	baseband
Medium	2 twisted pair cable
Range	500ft
Speed	$800 Kbs^{-1}$
No. of nodes	30

Compatible equipment: IBM PC and compatibles, Altos Systems.

Comments: PC Path is designed as a method of connecting IBM PCs into the Altos Team Net LAN and allows PCs to be used as terminals to Altos UNIX-based systems.

Plan 2000/3000/4000

Supplier: Zynar Ltd

Technology:

Topology	bus
Access	token-passing
Transmission	baseband
Medium	coaxial cable
Range	6600m
Speed	$2.5 Mbs^{-1}$
No. of nodes	255

Compatible equipment: IBM PC and compatibles, Apple II and III.

Comments: The Plan networks are produced by Nestar Systems in the US and are based on ARCnet (q.v.) together with operating software for the attached IBM and Apple equipment. Nestar and Zynar have been supplying LANs for some time (see Cluster/One) and their systems are based on a wide range experience in the LAN field. Basing the Plan Networks on ARCnet allows them to be run in conjunction with already-installed ARCnets although software compatibility is not assured.

Planet

Supplier: Racal-Milgo

Technology:

Topology	ring
Access	empty slot

Transmission   baseband
Medium   twin coaxial cable
Range   20km
Speed   20Mbs^{-1}
No. of nodes   500

Compatible equipment: RS232C devices.

Comments: Planet is based on a Cambridge Ring structure but varies from the Ring in some details. The twin coaxial cable allows Planet to isolate faulty nodes by turning the ring back on itself, thus making the system much more robust than a normal ring arrangement.

Plus Net

Supplier: Icarus Computer Systems

Technology:
Topology   bus
Access   CSMA/CD
Transmission   baseband
Medium   twisted pair cable
Range   1500ft
Speed   500Kbs^{-1}
No. of nodes   8

Compatible equipment: Sanyo 550, Sanyo 775, IBM PC and compatibles.

Comments: Plus Net is designed primarily for Sanyo microcomputers and also supports IBM PCs. An interesting feature is the provision for up to 12 separate file servers within a single network.

Polynet

Supplier: Logica VTS Ltd

Technology:
Topology   ring
Access   empty slot
Transmission   baseband
Medium   3 twisted pair cables
Range   100m between nodes
Speed   10Mbs^{-1}
No. of nodes   256

Compatible equipment: Logica products, DEC minicomputers, Intel Multibus equipment.

Comments: Polynet is an integrated office system based on the Cambridge Ring and differing only slightly from the standard. It is designed primarily for use with Logica's own range of business computers and has interfaces to popular minicomputer systems. Of interest mostly to people looking for a complete office automation package.

Primenet

Supplier: Prime Computer Inc.

Technology:
Topology	ring
Access	token passing
Transmission	baseband
Medium	coaxial cable
Range	230 between nodes
Speed	8Mbs^{-1}
No. of nodes	16

Compatible equipment: Prime computers.

Comments: Primenet is a networking system for Prime and other minicomputers, part of which is a ring-based LAN. For multiple Prime users, it is an obvious choice, but otherwise is probably not of general applicability.

Quadnet IX

Supplier: Quadran

Technology:
Topology	ring/star
Access	token passing
Transmission	baseband
Medium	various
Range	N/A
Speed	10Mbs^{-1}
No. of nodes	255

Compatible equipment: IBM PC and compatibles.

Comments: Quadnet IX is designed especially for use with IBM systems and uses one of the PCs as print and file server. Quadran supply complete systems including operating software compatible with Novell's Netware (q.v.).

Q-LINK/Quorum Net

Supplier: Quorum Computers

Technology:
	Topology	chain
	Access	token passing
	Transmission	baseband
	Medium	coaxial cable
	Range	600m
	Speed	500Kbs^{-1} (Q-LINK), 625Kbs^{-1} (Quorum Net)
	No. of nodes	8 (Q-LINK), 64 (Quorum Net)

Compatible equipment: IBM PC, Apricot (Q-LINK), Apricot (Quorum Net)

Comments: Quorum provide a range of networking solutions for microcomputer users. Q-LINK is designed for a small number of PCs running MS DOS and is based on a central file server. Quorum Net is a more wide-ranging and versatile system designed for up to 64 Apricots. Quorum also supply Q-LAN components, which are CP/M-based microcomputers which are Quorum Net-compatible. All systems contain hardware and operating software.

Ringway

Supplier: Vuman Ltd

Technology:
	Topology	ring
	Access	buffer insertion
	Transmission	baseband
	Medium	coaxial cable
	Range	N/A
	Speed	57.6Kbs^{-1}
	No. of nodes	99

Compatible equipment: RS232C devices

Comments: Ringway is a low cost ring-based network developed specifically for standard microcomputers and peripherals, hence the RS232C connection. Ringway is compatible with Clearway (q.v.) and can be mixed with it.

SILK

Supplier: Hasler UK

Technology:
Topology	ring
Access	register insertion
Transmission	baseband
Medium	coaxial/fibre optic
Range	200m
Speed	$16.896Mbs^{-1}$
No. of nodes	1050

Compatible equipment:. V.24 standard equipment.

Comments: SILK (System for Integrated Local Communication) was developed from one of the first true LANs and is designed, as its name suggests, to integrate voice and data transmission in the same system. Of interest to large scale users requiring both facilities.

Symbnet

Supplier: Symbnet Computer Systems

Technology:
Topology	tree and branch
Access	N/A
Transmission	baseband
Medium	fibre optic
Range	9km
Speed	$50Kbs^{-1}$
No. of nodes	N/A

Compatible equipment: Apple microcomputers, IBM PC, BBC micro.

Comments: Symbnet is part of a networking system from Symbiotic which includes file servers, tape back-up units, and network controllers. Symbnet's main feature is its use of optical fibre as the transmission medium, allowing it to be used in electrically-noisy environments, such as factories.

Synchro-Net

Supplier: Computer Communication Techniques

Technology:
Topolog
Access
Transmission
Medium
Range
Speed
No. of nodes‹c 3› Ring
Register insertion
Baseband
Twisted pair cable
1km between active nodes
125Kbs^{-1}
720

Compatible Equipment: RS232C devices.

Comments: Synchro-Net is a low cost ring network designed for use with a wide variety of hardware. Operating software is available to run under most popular microcomputer operating systems (e.g. C/PM, MS-DOS).

Techlan

Supplier: Canberra Instruments

Technology:

Topology	bus
Access	user-selectable
Transmission	base or broadband
Medium	coaxial cable or fibre optic
Range	10km
Speed	2.5Kms^{-1}
No. of nodes	unlimited

Compatible equipment: DEC Q-Bus, Intel Mulitibus, IBM PC, VME Bus.

Comments: Techlan is a high-performance LAN with a number of user-selectable variations making it suitable for most applications. The use of dual-redundant systems and bus isolation through transformers make it particularly suitable for industrial automation and the manufacturers are working towards full MAP compatibilty.

10 Net

Supplier: Techland

Technology:
Topology	bus
Access	CSMA/CD
Transmission	baseband
Medium	twisted pair cable
Range	1Mbs^{-1}
Speed	2000ft
No. of nodes	255

Compatible equipment: IBM PC and compatibles.

Toltec DataRing

Supplier: Toltec

Technology:
Topology	ring
Access	empty slot
Transmission	baseband
Medium	twisted pair cable
Range	5.5 miles
Speed	10Mbs^{-1}
No. of nodes	254

Compatible equipment: DEC Unibus systems, DEC Q-bus systems, S100 bus systems, IEEE-488 devices.

Comments: The Toltec DataRing is essentially a Cambridge Ring and is designed mainly for use with minicomputer systems. This is reflected in the range of interface units available. Operating software is also available.

Torchnet

Supplier: Torch Computers

Technology:
Topology	bus
Access	CSMA/CD
Transmission	baseband
Medium	twisted pair
Range	1km max.
Speed	330Kbs^{-1}
No. of nodes	254

Compatible equipment: Torch microcomputers, Acorn microcomputers.

Comments: Torchnet is Torch's implemetation of Acorn's Econet (q.v.) with added software and services which make it suitable for business and office automation use.

Transnet

Supplier: Transtec

Technology:
Topology	bus
Access	token passing
Transmission	baseband
Medium	twisted pair
Range	1km
Speed	N/A
No. of nodes	N/A

Compatible equipment: IBM PC and compatibles

Comments:

Transring 3000

Supplier: SEEL Ltd

Technology:
Topology	ring
Access	empty slot
Transmission	baseband
Medium	twisted pair cable
Range	N/A
Speed	$10Mbs^{-1}$
No. of nodes	254

Compatible equipment: DEC Unibus, DEC Q-bus, Intel Multibus, S100 Bus equipment, RS232C devices.

Comments: Transring 3000 is SEEL's implementation of the Cambridge Ring '82 standard, and is designed mainly for minicomputer systems. The various network components, including a 16-line terminal concentrator for RS232C interfacing are available separately. There is no networking software supplied. The terminal concentrator can also operate as a standalone star network.

Turbonet

Supplier: Equinox

Technology:
Topology	bus
Access	CSMA/CD
Transmission	baseband
Medium	twisted pair cable
Range	N/A
Speed	$800 Kbs^{-1}$
No. of nodes	16

Compatible equipment: IBM PC and compatibles, Equinox equipment.

Comments: Turbonet is a LAN for IBM PCs based on the Equinox file server unit. Turbonets can be linked together to form larger networks.

Usernet

Supplier: Sperry UK

Technology:
Topology	bus
Access	CSMA/CD
Transmission	baseband
Medium	coaxial cable
Range	1.2km
Speed	$1 Mbs^{-1}$
No. of nodes	64

Compatible equipment: IBM PC and compatibles, Sperry PC.

Comments: Sperry's Usernet is a version of Omninet (q.v.) for use primarily with their own PCs. Operating software is based on Novell's (q.v.).

U-Net

Supplier: U-Microcomputers

Technology:
Topology	star
Access	N/A
Transmission	baseband

Medium	RS232C cable (six core)
Range	50ft each arm
Speed	9600b s^{-1} max.
No. of nodes	29

Compatible equipment: Apple equipment, BBC Micro.

Comments: U-Net is a low cost star network designed initially for use with 6502-based devices e.g. Apple II and BBC Model 'B'. The net controller provides file-print-serving and can be an Apple II or U-Micro's own U-Net controller. Software is available for all supported hardware.

V-Net

Supplier: Format PC

Technology:

Topology	star
Access	time division multiplex
Transmission	baseband
Medium	RS232C cable
Range	RS232C standard
Speed	9600 Band max.
No. of nodes	32

Compatible equipment: RS232C devices.

Comments: V-Net is a low cost LAN with wide applicability and is discussed fully in Chapter 8.

VLSI 1553-NET

Supplier: Accent

Technology:

Topology	bus
Access	CSMA/CD
Transmission	baseband
Medium	coaxial cable or twisted pair
Range	4000ft
Speed	3Mb s^{-1}
No. of nodes	254

Compatible equipment: IBM PC and compatibles, Apple II series, S100 Bus systems.

Comments: VLSI Networks' 1553-Net LAN is designed primarily for microcomputers and provides the necessary operating software to run with the standard operating systems.

Wangnet

Supplier: Wang UK

Technology:
Topology	bus
Access	various
Transmission	broadband
Medium	twin coaxial cable
Range	6 miles
Speed	various
No. of nodes	unlimited

Compatible equipment: Wang equipment.

Comments: Wangnet is a comprehensive broadband networking system. It is intended for use with Wang office automation products but has frequency bands assigned for voice and video traffic, as well as a general purpose band available to other equipment for data transmission.

X-Net

Supplier: Christian Rovsing Systems

Technology:
Topology	tree
Access	N/A
Transmission	baseband
Medium	twisted pair coaxial cable
Range	4km
Speed	2-16Mbs [1]
No. of nodes	254

Compatible equipment: Virtually all microcomputers and terminals.

Comments: X-Net is a high powered LAN concentrating on the minicomputer area.

Xinet

Supplier: Xionics

Technology:
Topology	ring
Access	empty slot
Transmission	baseband
Medium	10 core cable
Range	400m between nodes
Speed	$10 Mbs^{-1}$
No. of nodes	512

Compatible Equipment: Xibus products, most minicomputers.

Comments: Xinet is part of Xionics' integrated system of office automation products and is intended to be used with them in conjunction with mini– and mainframe computers.

Z-Net

Supplier: Zilog

Technology:
Topology	bus
Access	CSMA/CD
Transmission	baseband
Medium	coaxial cable
Range	2km
Speed	$800 Kbs^{-1}$
No. of nodes	255

Compatible equipment: Zilog computers, RS232C devices.

Comments: Z-Net is designed primarily for use with Zilog's own range of equipment and can be supplied with operating software to run under UNIX.

Ethernet Systems

As well as the big three – DEC, Intel and Xerox – who provide Ethernet LANs, there is a host of manufacturers producing modules or complete systems which conform to the Ethernet/IEEE 802.3 specifications. The following list will not be exhaustive by any means, but will serve as a guide to the sort of products available.

Intel – OpenNET: A range of hardware and software products which can be put together to make an Ethernet LAN.

DEC – DecNET: Modular hardware and software based on Ethernet which can be used to produce a LAN for DEC equipment. Hardware includes plug-in boards and stand-alone units. Installation services are also available.

Xerox: Complete office automation system based on Ethernet.

Able Computer: Ethernet controller boards for DEC Unibus.

Ambar Components: Hardware: Unibus controller
Multibus controller
Hard disk server unit
Ethernet interface for IBM PC.
Software: Print server
File server
Electronic mail

Data Translation: The Interlan range of Ethernet products, including Net/Plus (q.v.)
Hardware and software covering most requirements

Sphinx: Bridge Communications range of Ethernet products including Ethernet Bridges, gateways to other networks, terminal servers with RS232C connections, and operating software.

Data Guild: Excelan range of Ethernet products including software to run under most popular minicomputer operating systems.

Advanced Micro Devices: A range of specialised integrated circuits for inclusion in Ethernet interface construction.

Interlekt Electronics: The Sension range of Ethernet components, including transceivers, repeaters, serial line interfaces and cable hardware.

Logic Replace-ment Technology: Multibus-based Ethernet controller

TSL Communications. Ethernet components as part of a wider networking product and service range.

Appendix B
Standards

The following publications contain information about the relevant LAN standards.

The Ethernet, a Local Area Network. Data Link and Physical Layer Specifications, Version 1.0. Published by DEC, Xerox and Intel.

Open Systems Interconnection — Basic Reference Model, Draft proposal 7498. Published by the International Standards Organisation.

Functional Requirements Document. Published by the IEEE Computer Society, Local Area Networks Standards Committee.

MAP Specification, Version 2.1. Published by General Motors Technical Center.

Appendix C
Bibliography

There are few books published dealing with Local Area Networks in general but those published in the UK by the National Computer Centre are probably the best references.

Local Area Networks, by K.C.E. Gee, published by National Computing Centre, covers the subject in great detail and is an invaluable source of information to anyone getting to know LANs. The NCC's state-of-the-art report on Local Area Networks is also a good, if brief, introduction to the subject but is only normally available to subscribers to the NCC's Information Technology Circle.

The best up-to-date information is normally found in technical magazines in the form of articles about specific projects and new developments. The following all contain regular articles on LANs:

Systems International published by Business Press International. *Computer Systems* published by Techpress Publishing. *Network* published by VNU Business Publications. *Computer Design* published by Penn Well Publishing. *Communications* published by International Thompson Publishing.

For general information on networks and related subjects, the following books are useful references:

Computer Network Architectures and Protocols. Edited by P.G. Green Jnr. published by Plenum Press.

Technical Aspects of Data Communications by McNamara, published by Digital Press.

Appendix D

Glossary of Terms

Access method: The means by which a network node puts information onto the network. The access method normally allows one node uninterrupted control of the network until it has finished transmitting its information.

Address: The means of identifying network nodes. Each node has a unique address which allows it to recognise information directed to it. These addresses are normally binary numbers as far as the network is concerned but often correspond to user-defined terms like 'Printer' or 'File', to make network addressing more straightforward for the user.

ASCII: The American Standard Code for Information Interchange. This code is a widely-recognised system for representing the normal alphanumeric character set (A-Z, 0-9, punctuation) as binary numbers. Virtually all manufacturers of computers and peripherals use this code as standard.

Baud: Equivalent to bit-per-second – 1200 Baud is 1200 bits per second.

Bit: Unit of binary numbering, either '1' or '0'.

Broadband: Broadband transmission is the transmission of a very high frequency carrier signal which is modulated by digital information. The information is extracted at the receiver by a demodulator. Because of the extra equipment involved, broadband transmission is more expensive than baseband but can cover greater distances and if different carrier frequencies are used, can accommodate more than one piece of information simultaneously in a single section of the network.

Bus: A network layout, or topology, where all nodes have access to the same section, or bus, of the network transmission medium.

Bridge: A link between two networks of the same type.

Byte: A group of 8 bits. One byte is a commonly used size of binary number for representing characters and numbers in computer systems.

CSMA: Carrier Sense with Multiple Access. CSMA is an Access method used in bus networks where all nodes wishing to transmit monitor the bus

(Carrier Sense) to ensure it is clear before transmitting. All nodes are connected to the bus and have equal access rights (Multiple Access).

CA: Collision Avoidance. A method used in CSMA networks to prevent two nodes transmitting simultaneously with the resultant collision and corruption of information. Before transmitting, a node reserves the use of the bus by a quick handshake signal.

CD: Collision Detection. Used in CSMA networks to optimise use of the bus. When two nodes transmit simultaneously, the resultant collision of information is detected by both nodes, which immediately stop transmitting and wait a random time before attempting a retransmission.

CATV: Community Antenna TV. A method of supplying TV signals to a large number of subscribers using only a single aerial. The connecting cables, signal boosters and other fittings are perfectly suited for broadband LAN applications and, due to mass manufacture, are relatively cheap.

CPU: Central Processing Unit. The central part of any computer system, the part which executes the program instructions. CPUs come in all sizes, from single integrated circuits to large boxes containing a number of printed circuit boards.

CRC: Cyclic Redundancy Check. An error checking and correction system used in Cambridge Ring-type networks.

Deterministic: Deterministic access means that all nodes have access to the network in a controlled or deterministic manner. All nodes are guaranteed some access within a certain time.

EPROM: Eraseable Programmable Read-Only Memory. See PROM.

Empty Slot: An access method used in Ring networks. An empty data packet, or slot, circulates the ring continuously until it is seized by a node wishing to transmit information. The slot is filled with data and marked 'full' by the node before being passed on to its destination. The slot is designated empty again when transmitter and receiver have finished with it, whereupon it can be used by any other node.

Frequency Division Multiplexing: The splitting up of the available frequency range into a number of separate sections, each of which can be used for continuous transmission by a single network node.

Fileserver: An item of equipment attached to a network node which is used by the network as a central filestore for programs and data. Normally a microcomputer with a hard disc.

Flag: One or more bits used to indicate the status of a particular item of equipment or data.

Floppy Disc: Usual term for removable disc memories in computer systems. The smaller size (5¼" diameter) are sometimes referred to as diskettes.

Gateway: A connection between two dissimilar types of network.

Handshake: The signals that pass between two nodes or devices to ensure the correct transfer of data.

Hard Disc: Usual term for fixed (non-removable) disc memories in computer systems. Normally a much higher capacity than floppy disc systems.

Hardware: General term for all the parts of a network or computer system, excluding only the operating programs and stored data.

IEEE: The Institute of Electrical and Electronic Engineers. The US professional body responsible for many of the internationally-recognised standards for networks.

Interface: General term for any hardware or software used to connect two or more pieces of equipment or software together.

ISO: The International Standards Organisation, responsible for the OSI seven-layer model (see OSI, below), on which most manufacturers are basing their network architecture.

ITS: Intelligent Terminal Switch. A device which can interconnect a number of different terminals or other peripherals, often used as the hub of a star network.

Kilo-: In the context of digital technology in general, kilo-does not imply 1000, but rather 1028 which is 2^{10} or, in binary, 10000000000. This is a convenient size for digital equipment and thus kilo– has been adopted to refer to it. It retains its usual value in terms of frequency.

LAN: Local Area Network.

Logical: A logical connection is one where there is not a single direct physical connection between transmitter and receiver for the duration of the transmissions. For example, in a packet-switched network, the packets making up a single message may take different routes, and are only joined together to reconstitute the message at the destination.

Manchester Code: A method of encoding digital data so that the transmitted information is self-synchronising under all conditions. This is important where transmitter and receiver do not share the same synchronising clock signal. In Manchester Code, every bit has a transition at its midpoint, so that a binary '1' is a low voltage followed by a high voltage, and a '0' is a high voltage followed by a low voltage. This allows a stream of identical bits – all '1's or all '0's – to be identified clearly by a receiving device without any external synchronisation.

Mega (M): In digital technology, Mega-, like kilo-, is a power of two, rather than a power of 10. Its value is 2^{20}. Again like kilo-, it retains its normal value (10^6) for frequency-related measurements e.g. MHz, Mbit/sec.

Mail: In LAN technology, the facility for one user to send a message to another user which is automatically stored by the receiving device and displayed on demand.

MODEM: MODulator and DEModulator. The device which allows equipment to use broadband networks by generating and modulating a carrier signal for transmissions, and demodulating received carrier signals to extract incoming data.

Multiplexing: The process of transmitting more than one set of information simultaneously over a single transmission medium.

Node: Any point in a network where external equipment gains access to the transmission medium.

Operating System: That part of a computer's software which is permanently resident during operation and supervises the activities of the rest of the software.

OSI: Open Systems Interconnection. The ISO's scheme to make all computer systems and networks compatible by having an established standard for interconnections.

PABX: Private Automatic Branch Exchange. Used by some manufacturers as the hub of a star network, the typical PABX covers the same area within an organisation as an equivaient data network, with the advantage of already having installed (telephone) wiring.

Packet Switching: A system for efficient transmission of data over networks. Data is split up into 'packets', which are sent to their destination over whatever route may be available at the time, only being reunited on reading their destination.

Parallel: Parallel data transmission involves sending more than one data bit simultaneously, to increase overall transmission speed. Usually involves a number of wires as the transmission medium, increasing cost.

Parity: The parity bit often attached to data bytes is a simple method of detecting single errors within the byte. When the number of '1's within the byte is even, the parity bit is also set to '1' for even parity, or '0' for odd parity, and vice versa if the number of '1's in the byte is odd. If the receiver knows which form of parity is being used, it can perform a comparison check and decide if any errors have occurred during transmission. This is only effective as long as no more than one bit is in error.

Physical: A physical connection is one where there is a fixed electrical connection between transmitter and receiver for the duration of the transmission.

Polling: A method of network control where nodes are instructed to transmit in turn, under the command of a master node.

Print Server: A node within a network configured to receive all data intended to print-out. Normally attached to a high-speed printer.

PROM: Programmable Read-Only Memory. See ROM.

Protocol: General term for the set of rules governing a particular data transmission.

RAM: Random Access Memory. Normally used to describe any semiconductor memory device whose contents can be altered at will.

Read-Only: See ROM.

Register Insertion: Or buffer insertion, as it is also known, is a form of network access used in Ring LANs. A node wishing to transmit loads a buffer, or register, with data and on detecting the end of a passing data packet, switches the register into the ring. The data circulates the ring and on successful return to the transmitting node, enters the register which is then switched out of the ring.

Repeater: A device inserted in the network transmission medium to boost the signal and re-transmit it to the next stage in the network.

Ring: A network layout where the transmission medium forms a closed circuit and data circulates in one direction.

ROM: Read-Only Memory. Term applied to semiconductor memory devices whose contents cannot be altered once they have been set. Programmable ROMs can be set by the user, unlike ROMs which can only be set at the factory. Eraseable PROMs can be cleared and reprogrammed with special equipment, but not while they are in use.

RS232C: A widely-accepted standard for serial data transmission, originally for modems, and now used by most computer manufacturers.

Serial: Serial data transmittion implies that data is sent, one bit at a time, along a single cable or other transmission medium.

Software: General term for the stored programs and data contained within a computer system.

Star: A type of network where each node is connected directly to a central unit which performs switching and interconnection operations.

Station: External equipment attached to a network node.

Statistical: Statistical access implies that access to the network is not guaranteed but is only probable within a certain time. CSMA/CD is the most common statistical access method.

System: General term for any grouping of hardware and software that operates together in a coherent manner.

Time Division Multiplexing: TDM is the process of dividing the available transmission time into sections so that all devices wishing to transmit can do so in sequence, one per time division, without collisions.

Third-Party: Anyone other than the manufacturer/supplier and the user. In this context, normally suppliers of add-on hardware and software, or alternative sources of equipment.

Token-Passing: Access method used in both ring and bus networks. A node can only transmit if it is in possession of a special data packet, or token, which is passed from node to node in a set pattern.

Topology: The shape of the network. The most common topologies are bus, star and ring.

Transceiver: Transmitter and Receiver. The part of a network node directly connected to the transmission medium.

Transmission Medium: The thing that carries the information between nodes. In most networks, this is normally electrical cable or fibre optic cable.

Tree: A variation on the bus network where the original bus split into a number of separate branches.

ULA: Uncommitted Logic Array. These are semiconductor devices which can be designed by the user to provide complex functions previously only available either with a large number of devices, or by expensive mass-manufacture of specialised parts.

VAN: Value-Added Network. A network which provides some service as well as interconnection. British Telecom's Prestel is an example.

V24: A standard for modem connection used by the computer industry.

WAN: Wide-Area Network. A network covering large areas, usually connected via radio or telephone links.

X25: A standard for packet-switching, which is relevant to LANs where interconnection with other networks is required.

INDEX

10 Net 156
20mA loop 40

Able Computer 163
Access method 17
Advance Net 125
Advanced Micro Devices 163
ALOHA 31, 76
Ambar Components 163
Amstrad Network 113, 126
Appletalk 107, 126
Apricot Networks 127
ARCnet 127
ASTNET 128

BabyNet 128
Baseband transmission 26
Bibliography 167
British Microcomputer Manufacturer's Group 121
Broadband transmission 28
Buffer insertion 25
Bulletin Board 74
Bus, token passing 20
Bus 2, 15

C-NET 132
Cable Stream 129
Cable tap 60
Cable, types of 33
Cabling 59
Cachenet 129
Cambridge Ring 22, 45, 46, 82
Carrier signal 27
Casenet 130
CATV 28
Centronics 63
Chain 130
Cheapernet 122
Chip sets 121
Circuit-switched 36
Cladding 35
CLAN 131

Clearway	91, 131
Cluster/One	131
Co-axial cable	33
Codex 4000	133
Collisions	19
Commodore	111
Comparison tables	53
Compatibility	56, 119
Components, costs of	57
Core	35
CRC	79
CSMA/CA	18
CSMA/CD	18
Cyclic redundancy check	79
Data Guild	163
DEC	163
Decision Net	150
DECNET	163
Digital Equipment Corporation	81
Domain	133
E-Net	135
EasyLan	134
Echo suppression	67
ECMA	45
Econet	87-90, 134
Elan	135
Empty slot	22
Ethernet Consortium	43
Ethernet frame	79
Ethernet repeater	80
Ethernet systems	162
Ethernet transceiver	80
Ethernet, specification of	77
Ethernet	44
Expandability	62
Fibre optics	34
File server	5, 49
Frequency division	17
Frequency-agile modem	31
Gateway	5
Glossary	169

Grapevine 135

Head end 30
Hi-Net 136
Hydra 136
Hyperbus 137

IBM PC Cluster 138
IBM PC Networks 103, 137
IBM PC-DOS 106
IBM Token Ring 138
IBM token ring 45, 47
IEEE 488 40
IEEE 802 43
Infaplug 108, 139
Information interchange 4
Insertion, buffer 25
Insertion, ring 25
Installation 59
Instanet 139
Intel 162
Intelligent teminal switch 52
Intelligent terminal switch 70
Interchange of information 4
Interlekt Electronics 163
Interlekt ITS 140
ISO 41, 119
Isolan 140

Keynet 111, 141

LAN, definition 2
LAN, types of 9
LAN/1 141
Laserwriter 123
Lincmaster 142
Localnet 142
Logic Replacement Technology 163
Logical ring 20
Loop, 20mA 40
Loop 11
LSI Net 143

M24R 143
Macintosh 107

Mainframe, linking to.................................. 50
Manchester Code 28, 78
Manufacturing Automation Protocol 121
Message-switched 36
Messaging.. 50
Met/Plus.. 146
Micro Prd/Net 144
Microlan.. 143
Micronet 800 74
Minstrel 144
Modem, frequency agile 31
Modem, RF... 29
Modem... 66
Multicore cable....................................... 33
Multilink... 96, 145
Multiplexing 17

Nectar Ring... 146
Net/One 145
Netware 147
Networking.. 7
Nimbus... 147

Octet.. 78
Office automation..................................... 81
Omninet.. 148
Open Net 149
OpenNET.. 162
Operating software 60
Orbis 148
OSI 40
OSNET 149

PABX, advantages of................................... 69
PABX, disadvantages of 70
PABX 11, 65
Packet collision....................................... 19
Packet-switched 36
Paperless office.. 6
PARC 76
PC Path 150
PC2PC.. 150
PCNet 150
Plan 2000/3000/4000.................................. 151
Planet 151

Polynet.................................... 152
Prestel..................................... 73
Primenet................................... 153
PrimeNet................................... 153
Print server............................... 5, 49
Process control............................ 50
Project Universe........................... 72
Protocols, high level...................... 85

Q-Link..................................... 154
Quadnet IX................................. 153
Quorum Net................................. 154

Register insertion......................... 25
Repeater................................... 12, 80
Research networks.......................... 75
RF Modem................................... 29
Ribbon cable............................... 33
Ring Monitor............................... 14
Ring, logical.............................. 20
Ring, token passing........................ 21
Ring....................................... 12
Ringway.................................... 154
RS232C..................................... 40

Seven-layer model.......................... 41
Signalling methods......................... 26
SILK....................................... 155
Slot, empty................................ 22
Specifying (a LAN)......................... 51
Speech..................................... 82
Sphinx..................................... 163
Standardisation............................ 63
Standards.................................. 39, 63, 165
Star network............................... 9
Symbnet.................................... 155
Synchronet................................. 156

Tap, cable................................. 60
Techlan.................................... 156
Technical and Office Protocol.............. 121
Telecom Gold............................... 73
Time division multiplexing................. 17
Token passing ring......................... 21
Token-passing bus.......................... 20

Token 22
Toltec DataRing 157
Topology 9
Torchnet 157
Transceiver 80
Transmission, baseband 26
Transmission, broadband 28
Transnet 158
Transring 3000 158
Tree 16
TSL 163
Turbonet 159
Turnkey systems 56
Turnkey 7
Twisted pair 32

U-Net 159
ULA 122
University of Hawaii 76
User requirements 49
Usernet 159

V-Net 106, 160
Value added network 73
VAN 73
Video 50
VLSA 1553-NET 160

WAN 4, 72
Wangnet 161
Wide area telephone network 72

X-Net 161
X25 Packet-switched network 123
Xerox Corp. 45
Xerox 163
Xinet 161

Z-Net 162